REWRITING *your* STORY

Compassionate and Practical Guide for Parents Navigating the Profound Pain of Estrangement

Books by Anna Strand

Abandoned Mother: Musings from a Mother of An Estranged Adult Child

Rewriting Your Story: Compassionate and Practical Guide for Parents Navigating the Profound pain of Estrangement

Living Your New Story: A Guided Workbook for Parents Healing From Estrangement

Rewriting Your Story: Compassionate and practical guide for parents navigating the profound pain of estrangemen

Copyright © 2025 by Anna Strand
Cover design copyright © 2025 by Anna Strand

All rights reserved. No part of this book may be scanned, uploaded, reproduced, distributed, or transmitted in any form or by any means whatsoever without written permission from the author, except in the case of brief quotations embodied in critical articles and reviews. Thank you for supporting the author's rights.

Printed in the United States of America
ISBN: 978-0-9675174-4-5
Year of first printing: 2025

REWRITING *your* STORY

Compassionate and Practical Guide for Parents Navigating the Profound Pain of Estrangement

Anna Strand

FORWARD

Has a rift with your child left you feeling lost, heartbroken, or invisible? Written by a parent who intimately understands your pain, *Rewriting Your Story* offers a compassionate and practical guide for parents navigating the profound pain of estrangement.

Parental estrangement is a unique grief, often compounded by silence, stigma, and a lack of resources. Author Anna Strand draws upon years of personal experience with estrangement and her work with other parents facing this unique kind of loss. Begin to understand the complex emotions that accompany this difficult journey—from confusion and blame to anger and profound sadness.

This isn't a book about reconciliation, though it doesn't rule it out. Instead, *Rewriting Your Story* empowers you to shift your focus from what you can't control to what you can: your own healing and well-being. Strand provides a roadmap to help you:

- Acknowledge and process the multifaceted grief of estrangement.
- Challenge self-blame and develop healthier coping mechanisms.
- Understand how self-compassion is vital for healing.
- Reclaim your identity beyond the parent-child relationship.
- Cultivate resilience and find renewed purpose and joy.
- Build a supportive community of others who understand.

Through insightful exercises, reflective prompts, and stories of parents who have navigated similar struggles, *Rewriting Your Story* validates your experience and offers a beacon of hope. It's time to release the narrative of shame and regret and begin crafting a new chapter—one where you are the empowered author of your own peace and future.

"A vital resource for any parent grappling with the silent sorrow of estrangement. Strand's empathetic guidance is a true gift." —Eleanor Vance, parent of an estranged adult child

CONTENTS

Forward iv
A Mother's Journey: From Devastation to Healing. 1
    Navigating the Depths of Estrangement 2
    From Grief to Purpose. 3
Chapter 1: The Unspoken Grief—Acknowledging the Rupture. 7
    Physical Manifestations of Grief 11
    Creating Daily Rituals. 12
    Moving Forward While Honoring Your Pain. 14
    Creating a Safe Space for Grief 16
    Building a Support Network 19
Chapter 2: The Weight of "Why?"—Releasing Blame and Shame. . . 22
    Understanding the Blame Cycle 22
    The Difference Between Responsibility and Blame 23
    The Impact of Societal Judgment. 25
    The Role of Cultural Expectations. 27
    Breaking Free from Self-Punishment 28
    The Power of Perspective-Taking 30
    Building Shame Resilience. 31
    Moving Beyond the "Why" 37
    Navigating External Judgment. 37
    Developing a Response Strategy 38
    Dealing with Family Events. 41
    Creating New Narratives. 42
    Looking Ahead 44
Chapter 3: Your Story, Their Story,
The True Story—Disentangling Narratives 46
    Understanding Narrative Perspectives 48

    The Science of Memory and Meaning 49
    The Generational Lens 51
    Your Story: Honoring Your Truth 51
    Validating Your Reality 52
    Emotional Triggers 54
    Creating a Balanced Narrative 56
    A Word About Therapy: 60
    Maintaining Your Truth While Listening to Your Child 61
    Practical Tools for Navigating Different Narratives 64
    Communication Strategies for Narrative Work 67
    Developing Communication Guidelines 68
    Looking Forward: Integration and Growth 71

Chapter 4: The Power of the Pen—
Journaling for Discovery and Release. 74
    Understanding the Power of Therapeutic Writing 75
    Creating Your Safe Writing Space 76
    Getting Started with Journaling. 77
    Moving Beyond Basic Writing. 80
    Structured Writing Exercises 81
    Writing Through Different Emotional States. 87
    Exploring Forgiveness Through Writing 91
    Building Self-Compassion Through Writing 93
    Creating New Narratives. 94
    The Role of Regular Review. 97
    Writing Your Way Forward 98
    Key Takeaways: 99

Chapter 5: Reframing Your Lens—
Shifting from Blame to Understanding 100
    Understanding Cognitive Reframing 101
    The Impact of Thought Patterns 101

    Common Unhelpful Thought Patterns:.................. 102
    The Impact of Social Judgment..................... 104
    Creating New Thought Patterns..................... 106
    Building Resilient Thought Patterns................. 113
    Common Challenging Situations and Reframing Options:.... 114
    Daily Reframing Practice.......................... 116
    Creating Your Personal Thought Reframing Toolkit........ 118
    Common Challenges and Strategies.................. 119
    Working with Setbacks........................... 121
    Creating Supportive Environments................... 122
    Key Takeaways:................................ 127

Chapter 6: Cultivating Kindness—
The Practice of Self-Compassion....................... 129
    Understanding True Self-Compassion................. 131
    The Science of Self-Kindness...................... 131
    Getting Started with Self-Compassion................ 132
    Building Your Self-Compassion Practice............... 133
    The Power of Sensory Support..................... 135
    Breaking Through Common Barriers.................. 136
    Building a Daily Practice.......................... 137
    Creating Safe Spaces for Practice.................... 138
    Working with Difficult Emotions.................... 141
    Using Your Self-Compassion Tools:
    Working Through Challenges...................... 141
    Building Your Emergency Kit...................... 144
    Handling Setbacks............................. 144
    Remember Your Support Network................... 145
    Moving Beyond Words........................... 146
    Working with Deep Pain.......................... 146
    Integrating Self-Compassion into Daily Life............. 147

    Looking to the Future 148
    Embracing Self-Compassion as a Way of Life 150
    Key Takeaways: 151

Chapter 7: Setting Boundaries—Navigating the Present Reality . . . 152
    Understanding Healthy Boundaries. 153
    Creating Your Boundary Framework 154
    Building Your Boundary Tool Kit 156
    Navigating Social Situations: Finding Your Balance. 157
    Managing Digital Boundaries in a Connected World 159
    Managing Family Events 163
    Managing Birthday Boundaries 164
    Boundaries in Handling Major Life Events 165
    Boundaries with Your Estranged Adult Child 169
    Boundaries That Protect Future Relationships. 172
    The Power of Self-Compassionate Boundaries 174
    Finding Balance in Daily Life 175
    Moving Forward:. 176
    Key Takeaways: 177

Chapter 8: Acceptance and Hope—
Letting Go without Giving Up 178
    Creating Space for Hope While Honoring Reality. 181
    Building New Connections 184
    Creating New Meanings 186
    Building Resilient Hope 186
    Creating Your Hopeful Path Forward 189

Chapter 9: Writing Your New Chapter—
Reclaiming Joy and Building a Resilient Future. 191
    Understanding Resilience in Estrangement 192
    Creating Physical Space for New Beginnings. 192
    Finding Purpose Beyond Pain 194

Finding Joy 196
The Ripple Effect of Joy 198
Starting Small: The Micro-Moments of Joy 199
Resilience: Surviving to Thriving 202
Physical Wellness as Emotional Support 202
Creating New Traditions 204
Professional Development and Personal Growth 207
Planning for Your Future: Creating Vision with Flexibility 208
Creating Your Support Network 211
Embracing Your Continuing Story 213
Keys Takeaways: 215

Chapter 10: Beyond the Silence—
Legacy, Estrangement, and Peace of Mind 217
Financial Planning with Flexibility 218
Estate Planning and Legacy Considerations 219
The Myth of Unconditional Love 220
Self-Compassion 220
Different Estate Strategies 221
Emotional and Relational Considerations 223
Communication Strategies 224
Handling Potential Challenges 225
Permission to Change 226
Guardianship and Care Decisions 227
Digital Legacy Management 228
Legacy Building Beyond Traditional Family 230
Looking Ahead with Courage and Peace 231

Notes
Chapter 1 234
Chapter 2 234

Chapter 3 235
Chapter 4 236
Chapter 5 236
Chapter 6 237
Chapter 7 237
Chapter 8 238
Chapter 9 238
About the Author. 239

A MOTHER'S JOURNEY:

From Devastation to Healing

I AM A MOTHER OF SIX BEAUTIFUL children, and I carry the weight of losing one of them—not to death, but to something equally devastating: estrangement. The pain cuts just as deep, perhaps deeper, because somewhere in the world, my child is alive but unreachable, a ghost haunting the edges of my heart.

It happened without warning, like a lightning strike on a clear day. One moment we were a family, imperfect but whole, and the next, silence. No explanation. No goodbye. Just an empty chair at family gatherings and a phone number that would never ring with her voice again. The confusion was crushing—how do you make sense of something that defies all logic? How do you process the sudden absence of someone you carried beneath your heart for nine months and loved for decades?

The devastation that followed was unlike anything I had ever experienced. This wasn't the kind of grief that people understand or know how to comfort. There are no casseroles for estrangement, no sympathy cards for children who simply disappear from your life. The emotions crashed over me in waves—too volatile to contain, too deep to fathom, too permanent to accept. I was drowning in an ocean of loss, grasping for something, anything, to keep me afloat.

Life, which had once been filled with purpose and meaning, suddenly felt hollow. The simple act of breathing became a conscious effort. Colors seemed muted, food lost its taste, and even the laughter of my other children felt distant and muffled, as if heard through thick glass. I was utterly lost, wandering through days that felt more like a waking nightmare than reality.

Navigating the Depths of Estrangement

In my desperation, I tried everything. I wrote letters that went unanswered, sent texts that were either ignored or answered with cruel abuse, and reached out through family only to have my daughter lash out at them. Each attempt to bridge the chasm between us seemed to widen it further. Every word I spoke was twisted, and every gesture of love was met with volumes of abuse and cruelty that cut deeper than any physical wound ever could. The child I had rocked to sleep, whose scraped knees I had kissed, and whose dreams I had nurtured had become a stranger wielding words like weapons against my heart.

The isolation deepened when my daughter severed ties not just with me, but with our entire family. My other children, my husband, and my siblings were cast aside without ceremony when they wouldn't align with her agenda, which seemed aimed at pulling as many loved ones away from me as possible. Looking back, I recognized her pattern of regularly discarding friends and significant others throughout her life—most relationships lasting no more than a few years before she would simply walk away. But we were her family. We loved her unconditionally and kept trying, believing that blood, history, and shared memories would mean something more profound, something that couldn't be so easily erased. We were wrong. Our family gatherings became exercises in navigating around the gaping hole where she used to be—the missing piece that no one dared mention for fear of reopening wounds barely held together by hope and prayer.

Perhaps the cruelest twist was losing my granddaughter in the process—that precious little soul who had called me "Grandma" with such joy, filling my arms and heart with a love so pure it took my breath away. The silence from her absence echoed through rooms that had once resonated with her laughter. Every toy I couldn't buy her, every milestone

I couldn't witness, every hug I couldn't give became another small death in the ongoing funeral of our relationship.

There were nights when I truly didn't know if I would survive until morning. The darkness felt absolute, suffocating, inescapable. Sleep became elusive, and when it finally came, it offered no peace—only dreams of reunion that made waking feel like dying all over again. I questioned everything about myself, replaying decades of motherhood through a lens of doubt and self-recrimination. Maybe I was the monster others seemed to think I was. Maybe I deserved this agony.

The world seemed to have no compassion for parents like me. Society readily accepts that some parents are toxic, abusive, deserving of abandonment. The narrative is simple and satisfying: bad parents get cut off, good children protect themselves. But what about the parents who love deeply, who made mistakes but never stopped trying, who wake up every day wondering what they did wrong? We became the invisible grievers, the ones whose pain was deemed somehow less valid, less worthy of understanding.

Even when my husband held me as I sobbed, when my other children assured me of their love, and when friends tried to offer comfort, the voice of doubt whispered louder than their reassurances. Self-worth, built over a lifetime, can crumble in an instant when the foundation is shaken by profound rejection. I began to lose myself—not just as a mother, but as a human being worthy of love and respect.

From Grief to Purpose

Then I found something I hadn't expected: community. Online support groups became my lifeline, connecting me with other parents who spoke my language of loss and confusion. For the first time since the estrangement began, I didn't feel like an alien in my own grief. These were people who understood the specific agony of loving someone who had erased me from their life.

As I listened to their stories and shared my own, my perspective began to shift like sunlight slowly breaking through storm clouds. I started to see the situation more clearly and to understand that estrangement is complex, nuanced, and often inexplicable. I realized that healing was possible, even amid ongoing pain, and that I could choose to reclaim my story rather than let it be written for me by someone else's anger or rejection.

Some parents in these groups were newly wounded, their voices raw with fresh pain, feeling as though they had been pushed from a great height and somehow survived the fall—broken but breathing. Their stories reminded me of my early days of devastation, and I felt both compassion for their struggle and gratitude for how far I had traveled.

Others were in the middle of their journey, taking tentative steps forward while occasionally stumbling backward, learning to navigate life with one foot in hope and the other in acceptance. Their resilience inspired me, showing me that healing doesn't happen in a straight line but in a spiral that gradually moves upward, even when it seems to circle back on itself.

Still others had traveled further down this unwanted path, their voices harder and their hearts more guarded. Some had grown angry, bitter, and defensive—and as I listened to their stories, I understood why. When you reach out with love repeatedly and receive cruelty in return, when you exhaust every avenue of reconciliation only to be met with more walls, anger becomes a form of protection. But I also saw in their hardened faces a warning of what I could become if I wasn't careful—so focused on the injustice of my situation that I forgot to nurture the joy still possible in my life.

The more I learned, the more I realized that my healing journey required a delicate balance. I needed to process my grief and anger without letting them consume me. I needed to maintain hope without becoming trapped by it. I needed to accept the reality of my situation while remaining open to the possibility of change. Most importantly, I needed to remember that I was more than just a mother of an estranged child—I was a whole person deserving of happiness, peace, and love.

This realization led me to write my first book, *Abandoned Mother: Musings from a Mother of an Estranged Adult Child*. Through the lens of grief's familiar stages and in the form of short, poem-like reflections, I documented not only my own journey but also the shared experiences of countless parents walking this difficult path. Writing became both catharsis and connection, a way to transform my pain into something that might offer comfort to others drowning in similar darkness.

The response to the book was overwhelming. Messages poured in from mothers and fathers who had felt invisible in their grief, who found in my words a mirror for their own experiences. I created a Facebook page dedicated to offering inspiration for abandoned parents—small doses of hope and understanding to help carry them through the hardest days.

Eventually, the page evolved into a private group—a safe harbor for parents to share their stories without fear of judgment or attack. Too often, estranged adult children and their supporters patrol online spaces, ready to silence any parent who dares to express their pain or suggest that reconciliation might be possible. Our group became a sanctuary where healing could occur without interruption, where parents could admit their mistakes without being destroyed by them, and where hope could be nurtured without being mocked as delusion.

Through this work, I discovered a new purpose in life. Healing became not just my personal goal but my mission for every parent walking this lonely road. All parents—especially those of estranged adult children—deserve the chance to heal, to find joy again, and to reclaim their stories from the narrative of rejection and failure that society so readily assigns to them.

This understanding led to my second book, *Rewriting Your Story*, which focuses specifically on the journey toward healing and joy while remaining open to whatever the future may hold. In its pages, I've woven together my hard-won insights with wisdom from experts in trauma, grief, and family dynamics. I've included practical exercises designed to help parents process their pain constructively, along with composite stories from other parents at various stages of their healing journeys.

Some chapters and concepts overlap intentionally because healing is rarely linear, and the tools we need often serve multiple purposes at different stages of our growth. The exercises for managing shame might also aid in acceptance; the strategies for self-compassion can also guard against despair. I've worked to include what I believe are the most essential elements for transformation, knowing that each reader will take what they need when they're ready to receive it.

But perhaps most importantly, I want every parent reading this to know: you deserve to live a story that brings you joy. Your worth is not determined by whether your child chooses to have a relationship with you. Your value as a person extends far beyond your role as a parent, important as that role may be. You are not required to shrink yourself down to the size of your pain or to let estrangement become the defining chapter of your entire life story. For that very reason, this book isn't a roadmap to reconciliation but a path to joy.

The journey to joy is neither simple nor quick. There will be setbacks, moments of overwhelming sadness, days when hope feels foolish, and healing seems impossible. You will encounter well-meaning people who don't understand, holidays that feel hollow, milestones you can't share, and grandchildren you may never hold. The path forward does not erase these realities or minimize their impact.

However, finding joy is a goal you can achieve. I promise this not because I have reached some perfect state of acceptance or because my story has a fairy-tale ending, but because I have learned that joy does not depend on perfect circumstances. Joy can coexist with grief, hope can flourish alongside acceptance, and love can remain strong even when it is not returned.

You can rewrite your story. You can find meaning beyond the pain. You can create a life filled with purpose, connection, and beauty, even with this chapter of loss woven into its fabric. You are not broken beyond repair, and you are certainly not alone.

The story continues, and you have the pen in your hand.

Anna Strand

CHAPTER 1:

The Unspoken Grief— Acknowledging the Rupture

SARAH'S HANDS TREMBLE AS SHE SETS the Thanksgiving table, muscle memory guiding her through the familiar ritual. Eight plates, not nine. The absence of that ninth place setting screams louder than any holiday music playing softly in the background. For the third year running, her daughter Kari's chair will remain empty in the extended family gathering, the space a physical reminder of the void in her heart.

Later that evening, while scrolling through social media, a casual photo appears—Kari at a friend's Thanksgiving celebration, her smile bright and carefree. Sarah's chest tightens, her breath catching as that familiar wave of grief crashes over her. She quickly closes the app, but the image remains burned in her mind: her daughter living a life that no longer includes her.

If you've experienced a moment like this, you're not alone. The grief of parental estrangement often arrives in these unexpected waves, triggered by holidays, photographs, or even the most mundane daily activities. It's a unique form of loss—one that exists in a painful limbo between presence and absence.

Unlike the death of a loved one, where society acknowledges and validates your grief through established rituals and support systems, the loss of an estranged adult child often goes unrecognized. There are no sympathy cards for estrangement, no casseroles delivered by well-meaning neighbors, no standardized leave from work to process your pain. Instead, many parents find themselves navigating this profound loss in isolation, carrying a grief that few understand and many misinterpret.

Recent studies suggest that as many as twenty-seven percent of adults have experienced estrangement from a family member, with parent-adult child estrangement being particularly common. Yet despite these statistics, the topic remains shrouded in silence and shame. This silence only deepens the wound, leaving many parents wondering if their pain is legitimate or if they're "overreacting" to what others might dismiss as a temporary family dispute.

The truth is that estrangement grief is real, valid, and deserving of acknowledgment.

Dr. Pauline Boss, who pioneered research in ambiguous loss, describes it as:

> *"The most stressful kind of loss because it defies resolution and creates long-term confusion about how to grieve and how to cope."*

When your adult child is physically alive but emotionally absent, you're caught in an exhausting cycle of hope and despair, unable to fully grieve or move forward.

This grief often manifests in ways that might surprise you. You may find yourself:

- Rehearsing conversations with your estranged adult child in your mind.
- Scanning crowds for their face in public places.
- Preserving their room or belongings exactly as they left them.
- Experiencing anxiety around holidays or significant dates.
- Feeling triggered by seeing parent-child relationships in media or real life.

These responses are natural reactions to an unnatural situation. When the parent-child relationship—one of the most fundamental human bonds—is severed, it challenges our basic understanding of family, identity, and belonging. The pain you feel isn't just about missing your adult child; it's about grappling with a loss that touches every aspect of your life and sense of self.

Breaking the silence around estrangement grief often feels like the most challenging first step. Well-meaning friends and family members might offer platitudes that minimize your experience: "They'll come around eventually" or "It's just a phase." These responses, though often well-intentioned, can leave you feeling even more isolated in your pain.

Consider Maria's experience:

> *"At first, I couldn't talk about my son's estrangement without breaking down. When I tried sharing with my sister, she immediately jumped to problem-solving mode, suggesting I just needed to apologize or try harder to reach out. She didn't understand that I had already tried everything I could think of, even to the point of pleading. What I really needed was someone to sit with me in my grief, to acknowledge that this loss was real and profound."*

> **Common Grief Responses in Estrangement**
>
> ❖ Waves of intense emotions that seem to come out of nowhere.
> ❖ Difficulty concentrating or making decisions.
> ❖ Physical symptoms like fatigue, insomnia, or loss of appetite.
> ❖ Avoiding social situations or places that trigger memories.
> ❖ Feeling stuck between hope for reconciliation and acceptance of the current reality.

The impact of such dismissive responses often leads to what psychologists call "disenfranchised grief"—mourning that isn't socially acknowledged or supported. You might find yourself:

- Hiding your pain from others to avoid uncomfortable conversations.
- Feeling pressure to "get over it" before you're ready.
- Struggling to maintain relationships with friends who don't understand.

- Withdrawing from social situations to avoid explaining your adult child's absence.

Understanding the unique nature of estrangement grief is essential to beginning your healing journey. Unlike other forms of loss, estrangement grief carries a distinct emotional weight that can be difficult to name or fully process. Your adult child is physically alive but emotionally absent, making it difficult to process the loss fully.

One of the most challenging aspects of estrangement grief is its ambiguity. The lack of clarity surrounding the relationship can make it hard to find closure. Questions may linger—Is this permanent? Will things ever change?—and these uncertainties can lead to ongoing emotional turmoil. Without a clear endpoint, the grieving process is often prolonged and confusing.

> **What Not to Say to Yourself**
>
> ❖ "I must be a terrible parent."
> ❖ "If I had just done things differently."
> ❖ "I should be handling this better."
> ❖ "Other parents don't struggle this much."
> ❖ "I don't deserve to feel this way."

Another defining feature is its cyclical nature. Emotions can swing between hope and despair, especially during meaningful times such as birthdays, holidays, or milestones. Even hearing news about your adult child from mutual acquaintances can reopen wounds you thought had begun to heal. These recurring emotional surges can make the grief feel fresh again, no matter how much time has passed. Recognizing these patterns can be the first step toward understanding and managing the unique grief caused by estrangement.

Secondary Losses: Beyond the primary loss of the relationship, you may experience:

- Loss of identity as an active parent.
- Loss of anticipated future experiences.
- Loss of extended family connections.
- Loss of confidence in your parenting abilities.
- Loss of social connections who don't understand.

This type of grief involves multiple layers of loss. Parents aren't just grieving the current absence of their adult child—they're grieving the loss of their expected future, their role as a grandparent, their sense of family completeness. Each of these secondary losses deserves its own acknowledgment and processing.

Let's pause here for a moment to introduce an important exercise that can help you begin mapping your emotional landscape:

EXERCISE: Emotion Mapping Journal

Take a few minutes each day to note:

1. What emotions you're experiencing
2. What triggered these feelings
3. Where you feel these emotions in your body
4. Any thoughts or memories that arise

This simple practice helps create awareness of your grief patterns and provides valuable insights for your healing journey. Remember, there's no "right" way to feel— all your emotions are valid responses to this profound loss.

As you begin to acknowledge and map your grief, it's essential to understand that healing doesn't mean forgetting or "moving on." Instead, it means learning to carry your pain in a way that allows you to continue living while honoring the great depth of your loss.

Physical Manifestations of Grief

Estrangement-related grief can manifest in the body just as powerfully as it does in the heart. Parents navigating the pain of separation from their children often experience tangible physical effects—fatigue, muscle tension, headaches, and even changes in appetite or sleep. These symptoms are not imagined or exaggerated; they are genuine physiological responses to prolonged emotional stress.

Research by Dr. Kylie Agllias, social work researcher and educator, demonstrates:

> *"Estrangement can manifest in physical symptoms, including sleep disruption, changes in eating patterns, and increased susceptibility to illness. Understanding these physical manifestations helps validate the very real impact of emotional distress on bodily well-being."*

The mind-body connection during estrangement grief is powerful. Many parents experience:

- Chronic tension headaches
- Digestive issues
- Changed sleeping patterns
- Weakened immune system
- Heart palpitations
- Muscle tension and pain

Signs You May Need Additional Support

- Persistent sleep disruption.
- Significant changes in appetite.
- Difficulty maintaining daily routines.
- Increased physical ailments.
- Thoughts of self-harm.
- Inability to focus on work or relationships.

Creating Daily Rituals

Recognizing the link between emotional turmoil and bodily well-being allows you to better care for yourself. For parents feeling overwhelmed or unwell, this understanding can be an important cue to seek help. Whether it's speaking with a therapist, visiting a healthcare provider, or simply allowing yourself to rest, acknowledging these signs is an important step toward healing and reclaiming stability.

Small, intentional grounding practices serve as powerful stabilizing forces when life feels chaotic or emotionally overwhelming. These might be as simple as taking three deep breaths while focusing on the sensation of air entering and leaving your body or placing your hand on your heart and feeling its steady rhythm.

The key is that these practices are deliberately chosen and easily accessible—perhaps stepping outside to feel your feet on the ground, naming five things you can see around you, or repeating a calming phrase that resonates with you. What makes these moments transformative isn't their complexity, but their consistency and your conscious decision to pause and reconnect with the present moment. When your mind is racing or emotions feel too big to handle, these small rituals create a bridge back to your center, offering a sense of control and grounding that reminds you that this overwhelming feeling is temporary and manageable.

Consider developing one or more of the following:

Morning Acknowledgment

Start each day by allowing yourself one minute to acknowledge your feelings without judgment. This brief moment of self-awareness can help prevent emotional buildup.

Comfort Corner

Designate a specific space in your home where you can retreat when grief surfaces. Stock it with:

- Comfortable seating
- Soothing items (blanket, photos, meaningful objects)
- Journal and pen
- Calming activities (puzzle books, crafts, music)

> ### Quick Grounding Exercise
>
> When grief feels overwhelming:
> - Plant your feet firmly on the ground.
> - Take three slow, deep breaths.
> - Name five things you can see.
> - Identify four things you can touch.
> - Listen for three different sounds.
> - Notice two things you can smell.
> - Observe one thing you can taste.

Evening Release

End each day with a simple ritual of letting go, such as:

- Writing down one challenging moment and one moment of peace
- Taking a mindful walk

- Practicing gentle stretching
- Listening to calming music

Not that some rituals are better suited to weekly, monthly, or seasonal practice rather than daily repetition. Adding these is also important. What matters most is finding rituals that bring you peace.

Healing Rituals:

- Lighting a candle on significant dates
- Writing monthly letters (kept private or shared when appropriate)
- Creating art that expresses your emotions
- Developing new holiday traditions that honor both presence and absence

Creating meaningful rituals can provide structure and comfort during times of profound loss. Remember, these practices don't have to be elaborate—their power lies in their intentionality and personal significance.

Moving Forward While Honoring Your Pain

The journey through estrangement grief isn't linear. Some days, you might feel stronger, more capable of facing the world; other days, the smallest reminder can bring you back to that raw place of loss. Both experiences are valid parts of your healing journey.

Patricia, a mother of two estranged adult children, shares:

> "I used to think I was doing something wrong because I couldn't 'get over it.' My therapist helped me understand that healing doesn't mean forgetting. Now I focus on

---

Emotional Flexibility in Practice

❖ Loving your adult child while setting boundaries for yourself.

❖ Hoping for reconciliation while building a meaningful life now.

❖ Acknowledging pain while remaining open to joy.

❖ Accepting the current reality while maintaining hope.

❖ Honoring the past while creating new traditions.

building a life that holds both my love for my children and my commitment to my own well-being."

This dual reality—maintaining hope while living fully in the present—is one of the most challenging aspects of estrangement grief. It requires developing what psychologists call "emotional flexibility"—the ability to hold seemingly contradictory feelings simultaneously.

EXERCISE: Grief Expression Letter

Writing an unsent letter to your adult child can be a powerful tool that allows you to express all the emotions you've been carrying—whether it's disappointment, love, frustration, regret, or hope—without the pressure of crafting the perfect response or worrying about their reaction. This private space gives you permission to be completely honest about your feelings, to say things you might never feel comfortable sharing directly, and to work through complex emotions that may have been building up over months or years. The act of putting pen to paper or fingers to keyboard can help clarify your thoughts, provide emotional release, and offer a sense of closure that enables you to move forward in your relationship from a healthier place. Since this letter is solely for your own healing and self-reflection, you have complete freedom to write without filters, knowing that no one else will ever read these words unless you choose to share them—and you never have to.

Guidelines:

1. Find a private, quiet space.
2. Set a timer for 15-20 minutes.
3. Write freely without editing.
4. Express your feelings honestly.
5. Include both pain and love.
6. When finished, store or dispose of the letter intentionally.

> After writing, take time to practice self-care. You've done important emotional work that deserves gentle acknowledgment. Consider small acts of physical comfort like wrapping up in a blanket, enjoying a warm bath or cup of tea, or grounding yourself through gentle movement such as stretching, walking in nature, or simply stepping outside. These actions help signal to your nervous system that you're safe and held.
>
> You might also benefit from a creative or emotional release—listening to music that resonates, making low-effort art, or cooking. If connection feels right, reach out to someone who can hold space for you, whether that's a friend, therapist, or even a pet. Most importantly, give yourself permission to rest without pressure to fix or analyze.

Creating a Safe Space for Grief

Before healing can begin, grief needs a place to land. When the loss of a child comes not from death but from estrangement, many parents instinctively silence their pain—tucking it away to protect others or to shield themselves from judgment. But unspoken grief doesn't disappear; it accumulates. It settles into your body, your thoughts, and your relationships, growing heavier over time. Without a safe outlet, even ordinary moments can become emotionally loaded, as if the silence itself is amplifying the ache.

Creating a safe space for your grief isn't just a metaphor—it's a tangible and necessary act. Whether it's a private journal, a trusted confidant, a therapist's office, or a quiet corner in your home, having a dedicated space to acknowledge and express your emotions is essential. This is where healing begins—not with answers, but with honesty. By allowing yourself to *name* what you feel without filtering, minimizing, or explaining it away, you begin to reclaim the inner ground that grief often erodes.

Consider Thomas's story:

> *"For months, I kept my son's estrangement a secret from everyone except my wife. When colleagues asked about him, I'd mumble vague responses about him being busy with work. But the weight of carrying this silence became unbearable. Finally, I confided in my closest friend during our weekly coffee meet-up. To my surprise, he shared that his sister hadn't spoken to their family in years. That simple moment of connection helped me feel less alone."*

Keeping the truth from even those closest to us is a common initial response to estrangement. One parent I worked with didn't tell her husband about her new break with their daughter for an entire year. Tensions were already high between her husband and daughter, who had been estranged for the previous five years, and she feared that sharing the additional estrangement would only make things worse. But when she reached a point of utter desperation, she finally opened up. To her surprise, his understanding—shaped by his own experience with estrangement—became a lifeline.

Finding safe people and places to express your grief is crucial. These are individuals who can:

- Listen without trying to fix the situation.
- Validate your feelings without judgment.
- Respect your boundaries around discussing the estrangement.
- Offer support without demanding details.
- Stand witness to your pain without becoming overwhelmed by it.

EXERCISE: Safe Person Identification Worksheet

1. List potential support people in your life:

2. Consider these questions for each person:

- Do they respect my privacy?

- Can they sit with difficult emotions?

- Do they avoid giving unsolicited advice?

- Do they make me feel heard and understood?

3. Note specific ways each person might offer support:

> 4. Plan how and what to share with them:

Remember, not everyone needs to know everything. It's okay to choose different levels of sharing with different people in your life. Sometimes, the people we expect to be most supportive aren't prepared for the intense emotions or able to offer the kind of support we desperately need during estrangement.

For example, I opened up to my sister—someone I considered my best friend—expecting her full support. But not long after, she hosted a party for her granddaughter and didn't invite me because my daughter had said she wouldn't attend or bring my granddaughter if I was going to be there. My sister told me ahead of time what they planned and even apologized, but it still hurt deeply. I felt betrayed and abandoned. In fact, it was the lowest emotional point of the estrangement—a moment when, for the first time, I seriously considered acting on my lack of will to live. Only the support of my husband and the needs of my other children got me through that dark time.

Later, when my daughter's behavior worsened and my sister confronted her about it, my daughter cut ties with her too. While my sister and I still maintain a good relationship today, I don't share as much with her because I don't feel emotionally safe in the same way I once did.

Building a Support Network

While some relationships may feel strained during estrangement, this period can also reveal unexpected sources of support and connection. Friends, extended family, support groups, or even new acquaintances may step in with compassion and understanding. You may find comfort in shared experiences with others who have walked a similar path, helping you feel less alone. Though the absence of your child may be deeply painful, this time can also foster resilience and highlight the quiet strength of relationships you might not have otherwise leaned on. Consider expanding your current support network with the suggestions below.

Professional Support:

- Therapists specializing in family estrangement.
- Support groups for parents of estranged adult children.
- Grief counselors who understand ambiguous loss.

Peer Support:

- Online communities for estranged parents.
- Local support groups.
- Trusted friends who can hold space for your experience.

Self-Support:

- Regular self-care practices.
- Emotional regulation techniques.
- Mindfulness and grounding exercises.

Online support groups can be a lifeline in the early stages of estrangement grief. In those raw, disoriented moments when you feel like no one in your immediate circle and possibly understand, these virtual communities offer instant connection. You can log in at midnight, pour your heart out without fear of judgment, and receive words of empathy from someone halfway across the world who knows *exactly* what you're going through. I found these groups to be especially helpful during the times I felt most alone—when the silence in my home was too loud, or when a photo or memory reopened a wound I thought had closed.

There's something uniquely comforting about speaking with others who don't need background explanations or disclaimers. They *get it*. They've lived it. And within that shared language of grief and loss, it becomes possible to breathe a little easier, even if just for a moment.

But while online groups offer validation and a much-needed sense of belonging, it's also important to recognize when they've served their purpose. Over time, I realized that constantly revisiting stories of pain—while initially reassuring—sometimes held me in place. True healing eventually requires movement, not just understanding. It means building a life that makes room for joy and meaning again, even if the ache of estrangement remains.

Support groups for parents of estranged adult children can be a powerful starting point—a steadying hand when you're just beginning to find your footing. They offer a kind of immediate understanding and relief that few other resources can match. But as time goes on, healing invites you to take the next steps—to walk forward toward deeper connection, self-compassion, and a renewed sense of identity that isn't solely defined by what was lost.

Remember that acknowledging your grief is not a sign of weakness—it's an act of courage and self-compassion. By giving yourself permission to feel the full depth of your loss, you create space for healing to begin.

In the next chapter, we'll explore how to move beyond the crushing weight of blame and shame, starting the gentle process of releasing these burdens while maintaining hope for the future.

National Crisis Hotline

If you're experiencing thoughts of self-harm or feeling overwhelmed call:

988
or
1-800-273-8255

Available 24/7 for support and guidance.

Remember: You deserve support during this challenging time.

CHAPTER 2:

The Weight of "Why?" — Releasing Blame and Shame

LINDA STANDS IN THE GROCERY STORE, frozen in place. Two aisles over, a mother and adult daughter laugh together as they shop, their easy affection on display. Her chest tightens as familiar thoughts flood in: "If I had listened more . . ." "If I hadn't been so strict . . ." "If I hadn't given her so much . . ." "If I had just . . ." The items in her basket suddenly feel too heavy to carry.

Later at home, she finds herself once again scrolling through old photos on her phone, analyzing every expression, every moment, searching for the signs she must have missed. The weight of these questions has become a constant companion, as familiar as it is crushing.

If you recognize yourself in Linda's experience, you're facing one of the most challenging aspects of parental estrangement: the endless cycle of blame, shame, and questioning that can consume your thoughts and drain your emotional energy.

Understanding the Blame Cycle

The human mind naturally seeks explanations for painful experiences. When faced with the profound loss of an adult child's presence, the question "Why?" becomes almost unavoidable. This search for answers often turns inward, transforming into a relentless self-examination that can border on self-persecution.

Research has shown that parents often get caught in an exhausting cycle of analyzing past events, searching for answers. While this is a natural response, this pattern of self-blame and endless questioning typically impedes healing rather than promoting it.

The difficult truth is that estrangement rarely has a single, clear cause. Family relationships are complex tapestries woven from countless interactions, generational patterns, and individual experiences. While it's natural to seek a definitive explanation, this search can become a form of self-punishment that keeps you trapped in pain.

> **Common Self-Blame Thoughts**
> - "I must have failed completely as a parent."
> - "If I had done X differently, this wouldn't have happened."
> - "I should have seen this coming."
> - "Everything was my fault."
> - "I don't deserve to be happy while my child is gone."

Consider Michael's story:

> *"For the first year after my son stopped speaking to me, I spent hours every night replaying every argument, every decision, every moment of discipline. I was convinced that if I could just pinpoint the exact moment everything went wrong, I could somehow fix it. What I didn't realize was that this obsessive searching was actually preventing me from dealing with my grief and moving forward."*

The Difference Between Responsibility and Blame

One of the most crucial distinctions we can make in the aftermath of estrangement—or in any emotionally charged situation—is the difference between taking responsibility and accepting blame. While they may seem similar on the surface, their effects on healing, self-understanding, and future connection are profoundly different.

Responsibility is rooted in growth. It involves recognizing our actions, words, or choices and how they may have affected others, even unintentionally. It calls for reflection, not punishment. Responsibility allows us to stay grounded in our values, to learn from the past, and to remain open to change without drowning in self-recrimination.

Blame, by contrast, is often driven by fear, shame, or the need for control. It seeks a culprit—someone to hold accountable in a punitive way, whether ourselves or someone else. Blame rarely leads to clarity or reconciliation. Instead, it tends to shut down curiosity and compassion, replacing them with defensiveness or internalized shame.

It's important to remember that acknowledging imperfect moments—which all parents have—doesn't mean taking on the entire weight of the estrangement. The goal isn't to find fault but to find understanding.

In other words, healing doesn't come from assigning blame but from expanding perspective. Compassion—for yourself and others—is the necessary lens.

Consider this framework for examining past events:

Blame asks: "What did I do wrong?"
Responsibility asks: "What can I learn from this?"

Blame says: "I'm a terrible parent."
Responsibility says: "I did the best I could with what I knew at the time."

Blame demands: "I must find the reason."
Responsibility accepts: "Relationships are complex."

This shift in language helps us reclaim agency. When we approach difficult situations through the lens of responsibility, we're empowered to respond with integrity, rather than being immobilized by shame or driven by the urge to fix what may not be fixable.

Understanding the emotional terrain of estrangement often means confronting difficult inner narratives—especially those shaped by shame and guilt. While these emotions are frequently confused, they serve very different psychological purposes. Guilt arises when we recognize that our actions may have hurt someone, and it often includes a desire to make amends or grow. It is tied to specific behaviors and can lead to constructive change. Shame, on the other hand, is far more corrosive. Rather than focusing on something we've done, shame convinces us that who we are is inherently flawed or unworthy. In the context of estrangement, parents may internalize shame in ways that silence their voice and erode their self-worth, believing that the separation is proof of failure. But shame distorts, while guilt clarifies. Where guilt can open the door to growth and empathy, shame tends to close it, trapping us in a cycle of self-judgment. Learning to distinguish between the two is not just an exercise in semantics—it's a powerful step toward emotional healing and self-compassion.

The Impact of Societal Judgment

Parents of estranged adult children don't just wrestle with private grief. They often carry the invisible weight of public scrutiny. Our society holds deeply ingrained beliefs about the sanctity of the parent-child bond—beliefs that offer little space for complexity, hurt, or boundaries.

Elena shares her experience:

> *"When people learn that I haven't spoken to my daughter in three years, their first response is usually, 'But you're her mother!' As if I hadn't thought of that every single day. These comments make me feel like I have to either defend myself or agree that I'm somehow monstrous."*

Common judgmental responses might include:

Recognizing Shame vs. Guilt

Shame says: "I am bad."
Guilt says: "I did something I wish I hadn't."

Shame is global: "I failed as a parent."
Guilt is specific: "I made mistakes."

Shame is paralyzing: "I don't deserve happiness."
Guilt can motivate growth: "I want to learn and do better."

Shame tells us we are unworthy.
Guilt tells us we want to change.

Shame tears us down.
Guilt can help build us back up.

- "Family is everything—how could you let this happen?"
- "There must be something you're not telling us."
- "Just apologize and make things right."
- "You need to try harder."

These well-meaning but harmful comments reflect society's discomfort with parent-child estrangement and can drive parents deeper into shame and isolation. Understanding this dynamic is the first step toward developing resilience against such judgment.

EXERCISE: Identifying Your Shame Triggers

Take a moment to reflect on and write down:

1. Situations that trigger

2. Comments that cut the deepest

3. Your typical emotional and physical responses

> 4. Your current coping mechanisms (helpful or unhelpful)

This awareness can help you prepare for challenging situations and develop more effective responses to shame triggers. Later, we'll discuss more about prepared responses and give some starting suggestions.

The Role of Cultural Expectations

It's important to acknowledge that shame around estrangement can be particularly intense in certain cultural contexts. Different cultures carry varying expectations about family relationships, filial duty, and parental responsibility. These cultural factors can either amplify or complicate the experience of estrangement.

In many cultures, family estrangement carries a profound weight that extends beyond the personal. In Asian societies, the concept of "face" and the importance of familial harmony can make estrangement particularly shameful. In Latino communities, where familial bonds are often central to identity, the isolation of estrangement may feel especially acute, while African American families may feel additional pressure due to historical forces that have threatened familial unity. For those with deep religious beliefs, estrangement can feel like a spiritual rupture, especially when doctrines promise eternal togetherness with loved ones after death. In such cases, the pain is not only emotional but existential, threatening the very hope of reunion in the afterlife.

Maria, a first-generation immigrant, shares:

> "In my culture, mothers and daughters are supposed to be inseparable. When my daughter cut contact, I not only lost her but felt like I had failed my entire cultural legacy. The shame was so deep I couldn't even tell my sisters back home."

Breaking Free from Self-Punishment

The cycle of self-blame often manifests in subtle yet destructive behaviors that, over time, can become automatic and deeply ingrained. This inner narrative—"I deserve to suffer"—can quietly influence daily choices, shaping everything from how we talk to ourselves to what we believe we're worthy of receiving. Breaking free begins with awareness: learning to recognize these patterns as symptoms of pain, not proof of failure.

These behaviors often develop as coping mechanisms but ultimately keep us stuck in a cycle of emotional distress:

Common Self-Punishing Behaviors:

- Denying yourself joy or pleasure—Feeling guilty for experiencing happiness, especially in the wake of loss or perceived failure.
- Isolating from supportive relationships—Withdrawing from others because you feel unworthy of love, support, or connection.
- Obsessively reviewing past events—Mentally replaying mistakes or regrets in an effort to rewrite the past or prevent future pain.
- Neglecting self-care—Abandoning sleep, nutrition, or movement as a quiet form of self-punishment.
- Accepting mistreatment from others—Tolerating harmful behavior as if it were deserved or earned.
- Avoiding activities that once brought happiness—Refusing yourself simple pleasures as a way to "atone" for past actions.

Research in family dynamics shows that many parents unconsciously believe that punishing themselves somehow makes up for perceived parental failures or might even help bring their child back. This self-punishment becomes a form of magical thinking that only deepens their suffering.

EXERCISE: Breaking the Self-Punishment Cycle

This gentle, reflective exercise invites you to interrupt the cycle and introduce a small but meaningful act of self-compassion.

1. Identify one way you've been punishing yourself. Be honest but kind with yourself—look for behaviors that may feel justified but ultimately harm your well-being:

   _____

   _____

   _____

2. Ask yourself:

   - What am I hoping to accomplish through this behavior?

     _____

     _____

   - Is it truly helping me—or just reinforcing my pain?

     _____

     _____

   - How is this affecting my emotional, mental, or physical health?

     _____

     _____

     _____

- What would self-compassion look like in this situation?

  _____

  _____

  _____

3. Choose one small act of self-kindness to practice instead. This might be letting yourself rest, reaching out to a friend, writing a forgiveness letter to yourself, or doing something enjoyable without guilt:

  _____

  _____

  _____

Breaking the cycle doesn't mean forgetting or denying past pain—it means choosing not to relive it every day through silent suffering. Healing begins the moment you believe you are worthy of it.

The Power of Perspective-Taking

While it's important to acknowledge your pain, developing the ability to step back and view your situation with greater perspective can help loosen shame's grip. This doesn't mean minimizing your experience but rather placing it within a broader context.

Consider these perspective-shifting questions:

- How would I respond to a friend in my situation?
- What would I say to a younger version of myself?
- How might this experience look five years from now?

- What would my wisest self say about this moment?

Sarah reflects:

> "When I started treating myself with the same kindness I'd show a friend going through estrangement, something shifted. I realized I'd been holding myself to an impossible standard of perfect parenting that no human could achieve."

Grounding Techniques for Shame Spirals—When shame becomes overwhelming:

- Place your hand on your heart.
- Remind yourself: "I am human and imperfect, like all parents."
- Take three slow breaths.
- Name three things you can see.
- Feel your feet connecting with the ground.
- Repeat a self-compassion phrase.

EXERCISE: Compassionate Observer Letter

Write a letter to yourself from the perspective of a compassionate observer who:

- Knows your whole story
- Understands your intentions
- Recognizes your humanity
- Holds hope for your healing

This exercise helps create emotional distance from shame while nurturing self-compassion.

Building Shame Resilience

Dr. Brené Brown's research on shame resilience offers valuable insights for parents experiencing estrangement. The key elements include:

- Recognizing shame and its triggers
- Practicing critical awareness

- Reaching out for support
- Speaking about shame with trusted others

Let's examine how each element of shame resilience can be applied to your situation as a parent experiencing estrangement:

Recognizing Shame and Its Triggers

Understanding your personal shame triggers allows you to prepare for and navigate challenging situations more effectively. For parents of estranged adult children, common triggers might include:

- Holidays and special occasions
- Family gatherings where others bring their adult children
- Social media posts showing parent-child relationships
- Questions about your adult child from well-meaning friends
- Receiving invitations that highlight your child's absence
- Events that exclude you in favor of your estranged child

EXERCISE: Trigger Awareness Log

Keep a simple log for one week noting:

- Date and time
- Triggering situation
- Initial emotional response
- Physical sensations
- Thoughts that followed
- How you coped

This awareness helps you identify patterns and develop proactive coping strategies.

Practicing Critical Awareness

Critical awareness involves examining the messages and expectations that fuel your shame. Ask yourself:

- Where did I learn that parents are solely responsible for adult children's choices?
- What unrealistic standards am I holding myself to?
- How do cultural or religious beliefs influence my shame?
- Whose voice am I hearing when I criticize myself?

Parents often unconsciously adopt unrealistic beliefs about how they *should* raise their children—beliefs shaped by culture, media, and their own upbringing. These expectations often paint an idealized picture that leaves no room for mistakes, emotional complexity, or growth. The pressure to meet these ideals can lead to guilt, anxiety, or a constant sense of falling short, even when doing their best.

Recognizing the origins of these beliefs allows caregivers to step back and question whether the standards they're holding themselves to are fair—or even attainable. By examining these assumptions with honesty and care, they can begin to shift toward more forgiving, supportive perspectives that prioritize presence and connection over perfection. Letting go of these impossible ideals opens space for authenticity, adaptability, and deeper relationships with their children and themselves.

Reaching Out for Support

Shame thrives in darkness and isolation, feeding on secrecy and the stories we tell ourselves about our unworthiness, but connection can be a powerful antidote to its corrosive effects. When we bring our shame into the light through authentic sharing with others, we often discover that our experiences are far more universal than we imagined, and the harsh judgments we've imposed on ourselves begin

> **Challenging Shame-Based Thoughts**
>
> **Instead of:** "A good mother would never lose contact with her child."
> **Consider:** "Many loving, capable parents experience estrangement."
>
> **Instead of:** "I must have failed completely as a parent."
> **Consider:** "Parenting is complex, and adult children make their own choices."
>
> **Instead of:** "Everyone else must have perfect relationships with their children."
> **Consider:** "Many families face challenges that aren't visible to others."

to lose their grip. However, it's crucial to be selective about where and with whom you share your experience, as not every person or environment will provide the safety and empathy needed for healing.

The key is finding trusted individuals who can offer genuine compassion without trying to fix, minimize, or judge your experience—people who can simply witness your story and reflect back your inherent worth. This might be a close friend, a therapist, a support group, or a spiritual advisor, but the common thread is their ability to create a space where vulnerability is met with understanding rather than criticism. By carefully choosing these connections and gradually opening up within them, shame begins to lose its power, replaced by the profound recognition that our struggles are part of the shared human experience.

In Chapter 1, we talked about building a personal support network. Now, we'll take that idea a step further by evaluating and refining the list of individuals we've identified.

EXERCISE: Creating and Evaluating Your Support Network:

Support Circle Mapping

Draw three circles inside each other, or write in the circles on the next page:

1. In the innermost circle, write names of people you trust completely.

    - Trusted friends who can hold space for your pain
    - Professional counselors or therapists
    - Support group members who understand estrangement

2. In the middle circle, list those who can offer limited support.

    - Understanding family members
    - Selective work colleagues
    - Spiritual advisors or mentors

3. In the outer circle, note broader support resources.

    - Online support communities
    - Educational resources
    - Self-help materials

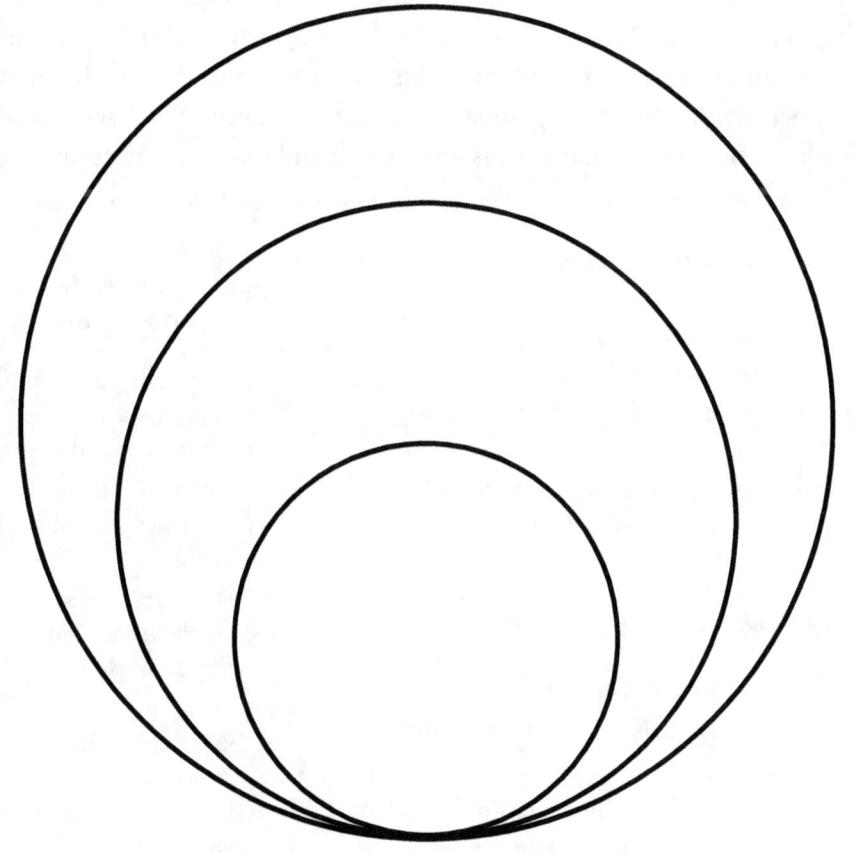

4. Use this map to guide your sharing choices.

Robert shares:

> *"Finding an online support group for estranged parents changed everything for me. For the first time, I didn't have to explain or defend my experience. Everyone there just got it."*

Speaking About Shame with Trusted Others

Learning to talk about your experience in a way that promotes healing rather than deepening shame takes practice, patience, and self-compassion. It often begins with recognizing that your story deserves to be told without judgment, even if your voice shakes or the words feel heavy at first. Over time, with safe listeners and intentional reflection, you can begin to reshape the narrative—not by denying the pain, but by speaking from a place of strength, understanding, and acceptance. This shift doesn't happen overnight; it's a gradual unlearning of silence and self-blame, replaced by honesty that affirms your worth and fosters connection. Let's take a look at some approaches to help you start sharing.

Productive Ways to Share:

- "I'm struggling with feelings of shame around . . . "
- "I could use support in working through . . ."
- "I'm learning to be gentler with myself about . . ."

Less Helpful Patterns to Watch for:

- Excessive self-blame.
- Seeking reassurance that reinforces shame.
- Comparing your situation to others.
- Minimizing your pain.

> **Signs You're Moving Beyond Shame**
>
> ❖ You can talk about the estrangement without feeling devastated.
> ❖ You're able to engage in activities you enjoy without guilt.
> ❖ You can acknowledge both challenges and strengths in your parenting.
> ❖ You recognize that your worth isn't determined by the estrangement.
> ❖ You can hold hope for reconciliation while living fully in the present.

Having a clear understanding of your support network allows you to navigate vulnerable moments with greater wisdom and care. When you know who genuinely listens, respects boundaries, and responds with empathy, you can share your experiences more strategically—offering the right details to the right people. This awareness helps you protect yourself from potentially harmful reactions such as dismissal, judgment, or exploitation. Instead of sharing broadly and risking unnecessary hurt, you can build trust deliberately, drawing strength from safe, affirming connections.

Moving Beyond the "Why"

While understanding is important, there comes a point when the endless search for "why" becomes counterproductive. Consider these alternative questions that can promote healing:

- What can I learn about myself through this experience?
- How can I grow stronger while honoring my pain?
- What would self-compassion look like in this situation?
- How can I create meaning in my life right now?

These questions shift focus from the past, which we cannot change, to the present, where growth and healing are possible.

Remember, moving beyond shame doesn't mean forgetting or dismissing your pain. Instead, it means creating space for both grief and growth, understanding and acceptance, hope and healing. Let's explore some practical strategies for navigating this delicate balance.

Navigating External Judgment

One of the most challenging aspects of parental estrangement is managing others' reactions and unsolicited advice. As an estranged parent, you're often met with confusion, judgment, or pity from people who assume you must have done something unforgivable. Friends and extended family may offer advice that oversimplifies the situation—urging reconciliation without understanding the years of tension, hurt, or miscommunication that led to the distance. Some may even suggest you're not trying hard enough, compounding the grief with blame. It becomes exhausting to constantly explain or defend yourself, especially when your pain is dismissed or treated as a problem to be quickly solved. The isolation isn't just from your child, but from a society that struggles to hold space for a parent's heartbreak without assigning blame.

Patricia, a mother of two estranged adult children, shares:

> *"The hardest part wasn't just the estrangement—it was dealing with everyone's opinions about it. Every conversation felt like a minefield, especially in the beginning. Sometimes I'd lie and say everything was fine, that we talked occasionally, just to avoid the looks."*

Patricia recalls how, in the early days after her children cut contact, the silence was unbearable—but what followed was almost worse. When she tried to confide in friends or extended family, the responses were rarely comforting. Some offered immediate advice, as if offering a simple fix she just hadn't thought of. Others looked at her with thinly veiled judgment, their expressions saying more than their words ever could. "What did you do?" someone once asked bluntly at a neighborhood gathering, as though parental estrangement could only happen in cases of neglect or abuse. Patricia had no answer that would satisfy them.

She faced similar judgment at work. "Well, you know kids these days," a coworker said dismissively. "They're just too sensitive." Another urged her to keep trying, to just show up at their homes unannounced, as if persistence would mend the damage. But they didn't understand the complicated history, the years of misunderstandings, unmet expectations, and emotional distance that grew like a slow-moving fault line.

More painful still were those who said nothing, who looked away when she mentioned her children, who quickly changed the subject. She felt like someone no one wanted to be around—as if her grief made people uncomfortable.

What Patricia wishes for most is not a solution handed to her, but simply someone to sit beside her in the grief without trying to tidy it up. She didn't need fixing; she needed compassion. Someone to say, "That must be so hard," and mean it.

Developing a Response Strategy

Having prepared responses ready can serve as a protective buffer, allowing you to maintain your composure and respond thoughtfully rather than reactively. These aren't scripts to recite verbatim but rather frameworks that help you stay grounded in your values and boundaries when emotions run high. Whether it's a brief encounter at a family gathering, an unexpected text, or a phone call that catches you off guard, knowing generally what you want to say helps prevent you from either shutting down completely or saying something you might later regret.

Prepared responses also preserve your emotional energy by reducing the mental load of constantly having to figure out how to navigate these difficult moments. Instead of spending hours replaying conversations or worrying about what you should have said differently, you can focus that energy on your own healing and well-being. Here are some starting points for you to consider.

For Casual Inquiries:

- "We're working through some challenges right now."
- "It's complicated, but I'm focusing on healing."
- "Thank you for asking, but I'd rather not discuss it today."

For Persistent Advice-Givers:

- "I appreciate your concern, but I need support rather than solutions."
- "I'm working with professionals who understand this situation."
- "This is more complex than it might appear from the outside."

EXERCISE: Creating Your Response Toolkit

1. List common situations where you face questions:

---

2. Write three possible responses for each.

   - Brief response (for acquaintances):

   - Medium response (for friends):

   - Detailed response (for trusted confidants):

3. Practice these responses until they feel natural.

Having these responses prepared doesn't make you cold or calculated—it shows you are protecting your well-being while still leaving space for healthier communication down the line, if and when it feels right.

Dealing with Family Events

Family gatherings can be particularly challenging when navigating estrangement. Planning ahead for emotionally challenging events is essential to maintaining stability and reducing stress. By developing a clear exit strategy, you give yourself permission to step away if the situation becomes overwhelming, preserving your sense of control. Equally important is identifying a trusted support person who can be available—either in person or remotely—to offer grounding, encouragement, or simply a safe space to decompress. Together, these preparations create a buffer against emotional strain, helping you navigate difficult moments with greater resilience and confidence.

> **Setting Healthy Boundaries**
>
> Remember:
> - You don't owe anyone an explanation.
> - It's okay to change the subject.
> - You can excuse yourself from uncomfortable situations.
> - Your healing journey is yours to share or keep private.

Melinda shares her experience.

> *"I went to a 4th of July event, excited to see my sisters and their families. Everything was fine until we got ready to head to the lake, like we did every year, and I couldn't find my mom. She'd put her things in my car, and since she was eighty and not in great health, my family and I searched her house and large backyard, fearing the worst. There was no sign of her. I called my sisters in a panic—only one answered, and she didn't know where Mom was. Then I found out Mom had left with the other sister. Instead of relief, I felt abandoned. Everyone had left me behind. Mom had chosen my sister, not me. I spiraled. It brought back the overwhelming pain of abandoned by my daughter all over again, and I wanted the ground to swallow me*

> *so I wouldn't have to feel the pain ever again. At the lake, Mom 'apologized' by saying she'd told her niece she was leaving—she'd confused her with one of my daughters. Later, the sister who drove her forcefully scolded me for upsetting Mom, said my reaction wasn't normal, and that I needed help. I snapped, 'Don't you think I know that? I just wish I could die.' Then I went upstairs and cried for hours. My sister never said another word except to blame me further. Even now, years later, she still doesn't understand. She doesn't even try. I've learned to protect myself whenever I'm around her."*

Strategies for Family Events:

Before:

- Decide how long you'll stay
- Plan responses to likely questions
- Arrange check-ins with a support person
- Give yourself permission to decline if needed

During:

- Take breaks when needed
- Use grounding techniques
- Focus on positive connections
- Remember your boundaries

After:

- Process your emotions
- Practice self-care
- Acknowledge your courage
- Reflect on what you learned

Creating New Narratives

As you work through shame and external judgment, it becomes possible to begin crafting a new narrative—one that honors both your pain and your resilience. You don't deny the difficulty of estrangement, but you refuse to let it define your entire story.

Experience shows that parents who heal most effectively are those who learn to hold two truths simultaneously: the pain of estrangement and their inherent worth as human beings."

EXERCISE: New Narratives and Self-worth

Complete these sentences:

- "This experience has taught me _____
_____"

- "Despite this challenge, I am _____
_____"

- "My strength shows in _____
_____"

- "I'm learning to _____
_____"

- "My hope for the future includes _____
_____"

Keep in mind that it's essential to recognize that this is an ongoing journey rather than a destination. Each small step toward self-compassion and understanding builds a foundation for deeper healing.

> Healing from shame is often unpredictable, marked by progress and setbacks alike. Some days, familiar habits or emotions may return, not as failures but as part of the journey. These moments don't erase the growth you've made—they simply remind you that healing takes time. What truly shapes your path is the steady intention to move forward and the willingness to treat yourself with compassion along the way.

Looking Ahead

As we move forward, remember that releasing blame and shame opens space for new possibilities. While the pain of estrangement remains real, loosening shame's grip allows you to:

- Engage more fully in present relationships
- Pursue interests and goals
- Find joy in daily experiences
- Build meaningful connections
- Develop a stronger sense of self

When parents learn to see their value as independent from the decisions their adult children make, they often uncover a deeper well of inner strength. This shift in perspective can bring a surprising sense of clarity and resilience, allowing them to support their children without losing themselves in the process. It's in this space of emotional separation that many parents find new confidence and peace.

In the next chapter, we'll explore how to understand the different perspectives that exist within every family story while maintaining your own emotional balance and truth.

National Crisis Hotline

If you're experiencing thoughts of self-harm or feeling overwhelmed call:

**988
or
1-800-273-8255**

Available 24/7 for support and guidance.

Remember: Seeking help is a sign of strength, not weakness.

Recommended Reading for Further Support:

- "Self-Compassion" by Kristin Neff
- "Daring Greatly" by Brené Brown
- "The Gifts of Imperfection" by Brené Brown

CHAPTER 3:

Your Story, Their Story, The True Story—Disentangling Narratives

BEFORE WE DIVE DEEPER INTO UNDERSTANDING different perspectives, let's establish an essential truth: experiencing estrangement does not make you a bad parent. The current cultural narrative often suggests that if adult children distance themselves, their parents must have done something terribly wrong. This oversimplified view ignores the complex reality of family relationships and the many factors that contribute to estrangement.

Dr. Joshua Colman, a specialist in family trauma, emphasizes:

> "Many estranged parents were loving, dedicated parents who did their absolute best with the knowledge and resources they had at the time."

Consider these important facts:

- Research shows that even exemplary parents can experience estrangement
- Cultural shifts have dramatically changed how parent-child relationships are viewed
- Social media and online communities can amplify and solidify grievances

- Mental health challenges, outside influences, and life stresses can impact adult children's perceptions
- Different generational expectations create natural friction

Research consistently emphasizes the value of understanding different perspectives, especially in parenting, where empathy and open-mindedness can foster healthier relationships and better communication. Recognizing that others may view a situation differently can lead to greater emotional intelligence and more nuanced decision-making.

However, it is equally important to acknowledge that this openness should not come at the expense of a parent's own lived experiences, intuition, or the effort they pour into raising their child. The ability to consider alternate viewpoints must be balanced with self-respect and confidence in one's unique parenting journey.

Invalidating a parent's experiences—whether through comparison, criticism, or internal self-doubt—can undermine their sense of agency and erode trust in their own judgment. Every family dynamic is different, shaped by personal history, values, and circumstances that outsiders often cannot fully grasp. While humility and learning are vital, so is honoring the wisdom that comes from being present in the daily, often invisible, work of parenting. Parents need to feel heard and validated, not pressured to erase or minimize their own reality in favor of someone else's narrative.

Consider Janet's experience: Janet sits at her computer, morning coffee growing cold beside her. On her screen, a Facebook memory has appeared: her

---

Truth vs. Trending Narratives

Current Social Media Narrative: "Toxic parents cause estrangement"
Reality: Estrangement is complex and multi-factored

Current Social Media Narrative: "Children only estrange for valid reasons"
Reality: Perspectives, interpretation, and outside influences play significant roles

Current Social Media Narrative: "Parents should just admit all their faults"
Reality: Understanding different perspectives doesn't require accepting all blame

daughter Rachel's sixteenth birthday party. In Janet's memory, it was a joyful celebration—the special dress they'd picked together, the chocolate cake with raspberry filling that took hours to make, the carefully chosen guest list. But Rachel's recent social media post about the same event tells a different story:

> *"That party symbolized everything wrong with my childhood—the controlling guest list, the dress I was pressured to wear, the perfect façade we had to maintain. #toxicfamily #boundaries"*

Janet's hand trembles as she closes the browser. How could the same event hold such drastically different meanings? Which version is true? And how can she reconcile her cherished memories with her daughter's painful ones? How could all her effort mean so little to her daughter?

If you've experienced a moment like this, you know the disorienting feeling of having your family narrative challenged. It can feel like standing on shifting sand, questioning not just specific memories but your entire understanding of your family's story.

Understanding Narrative Perspectives

Research in family psychology reveals that even siblings who grew up in the same household often have markedly different memories and interpretations of their childhood experiences. This divergence becomes even more pronounced between parents and children, who view family life from fundamentally different vantage points.

Why Memories Differ

- ❖ Emotional state affects memory formation.
- ❖ Age influences perception and understanding.
- ❖ Different roles create different perspectives.
- ❖ Cultural and generational factors shape interpretation.
- ❖ Personal needs influence what we remember.
- ❖ Present circumstances color past memories.

Dr. Kylie Agllias says:

> *"Family estrangement narratives are complex and multifaceted, with each family member potentially holding vastly different interpretations of shared experiences."*

Consider Thomas's experience:

> *"When my son cut contact, he sent a letter listing grievances from his childhood. One incident he described—a family vacation when he was twelve—I remembered as a happy time. But in his telling, it was filled with tension and disappointment. At first, I wanted to defend my version, to prove him wrong. But I've learned that both versions can hold truth, even when they seem contradictory."*

The Science of Memory and Meaning

Neuroscience shows us that memories aren't like video recordings that capture objective truth. Instead, they're complex constructions influenced by emotion, perspective, and subsequent experiences.

Dr. Daniel J. Siegel, an expert in brain development, believes:

> *"Memory is not a fixed recording but rather a reconstruction influenced by emotion, perspective, and subsequent experiences."*

This means that each time we revisit a memory, we're not simply replaying a mental recording—we're rebuilding it from fragments, influenced by who we are in that moment. Our current emotions, beliefs, and understanding all shape how we recall the past, subtly altering the memory each time it's accessed. This ongoing reconstruction can lead to strikingly different versions of the same event, especially among family members whose perspectives and emotional contexts may vary widely.

This understanding doesn't invalidate your memories or experiences. Rather, it opens the door to a more nuanced understanding of family history—one that can hold multiple truths simultaneously.

EXERCISE: Memory Mapping

Choose a significant family memory and explore:

1. Your emotional state at the time

   _____

   _____

2. Your role in the situation

   _____

   _____

3. What was happening in your life then

   _____

   _____

4. Your current feelings about the memory

   _____

   _____

5. How this memory fits into your larger family narrative

   _____

   _____

Consider how these factors might have influenced your perception and retention of the event.

The Generational Lens

Adding another layer of complexity is the significant shift in parenting culture and family expectations between generations. Many parents of estranged adult children were raised with values that emphasized obedience, self-sacrifice, and respect for authority, often without open discussion of feelings or boundaries. In contrast, today's younger generations are more likely to prioritize emotional safety, autonomy, and mental health—sometimes interpreting past parenting styles as harmful, even if they were well-intentioned.

This generational divide can lead to deep misunderstandings, as actions once considered loving or responsible may now be viewed as controlling or invalidating. Bridging this gap requires a willingness to acknowledge these cultural changes and approach the relationship with empathy, humility, and openness to learning.

Dr. Karl Pillemer explains:

> *"What constituted normal parenting practices a generation ago may be viewed very differently through today's cultural lens."*

Common generational differences in perspective often emerge around:

- Discipline methods
- Emotional expression
- Privacy boundaries
- Individual autonomy
- Communication styles
- Mental health awareness

Generational Perspective Shifts

Then: "Children should be seen and not heard."
Now: "Children's voices matter."

Then: "Push through emotional pain."
Now: "Acknowledge and process feelings."

Then: "Parents know best."
Now: "Children have agency."

Then: "Family loyalty above all."
Now: "Healthy boundaries are essential."

Your Story: Honoring Your Truth

While understanding different perspectives

is important, it's equally crucial to validate your own experience as a parent. Many parents, when faced with their adult child's different narrative, begin to doubt their own memories and experiences entirely. This complete self-doubt can be as harmful as rigid defensiveness.

Patricia shares:

> *"After my daughter accused me of being emotionally unavailable, I spent months questioning every interaction we'd ever had. I started to believe I must have been a terrible mother, despite the joy and connection I remembered. My therapist helped me understand that I could acknowledge my daughter's feelings while still honoring my own experience of mothering her with love."*

Validating Your Reality

Before we explore different perspectives, it's vital to anchor yourself in what you know to be true:

- The love you felt and demonstrated was real.
- Your intentions matter, even if impact differed.
- You made the best decisions you could with the information you had.
- Being an imperfect parent doesn't mean being a bad parent.
- Your memories and experiences are valid.
- You can acknowledge your adult child's feelings without accepting all blame.

Maria shares:

> *"My therapist helped me understand that I could validate my daughter's feelings about her childhood without invalidating my own experience as her mother. Both can be true—she might have experienced pain I didn't intend, AND I was a loving mother doing my best."*

EXERCISE: Anchoring Your Truth

Before examining different perspectives, write down:

- Three specific ways you showed love to your child

_____
_____
_____

- Two sacrifices you made for their well-being

_____
_____

- Three values that guided your parenting

_____
_____
_____

- Two moments of connection you clearly remember

_____
_____
_____

- Three parenting decisions you still feel were right

_____

_____

_____

This exercise is not about pretending you did everything right or brushing past the moments you wish had gone differently. It's about holding a steady, compassionate view of your role as a parent—acknowledging the full picture. When you approach the past with honesty and self-respect, you're in a stronger place to consider your child's perspective without being overwhelmed by guilt or defensiveness. This grounded clarity allows for genuine reflection, rather than losing yourself in blame or shame.

Emotional Triggers

Certain aspects of competing narratives can be particularly triggering for parents. Common triggers include:

- Accusations of intentional harm
- Dismissal of sacrifices made
- Rewriting of happy memories
- Claims of constant negativity
- Denial of love or good intentions

EXERCISE: Trigger Awareness

1. Identify your strongest emotional triggers:

_____

_____

2. Note your typical reactions:

   _____

   _____

   _____

3. Consider what these triggers say about your values:

   _____

   _____

   _____

   _____

4. Develop grounding techniques for triggering moments:

   _____

   _____

   _____

   _____

Family therapists often emphasize that when we become aware of what stirs our strongest emotions, we gain the ability to pause and choose how we respond. Recognizing these emotional triggers doesn't mean silencing your feelings—it means creating space between the feeling and the reaction. This space allows for calmer, more intentional communication, even in the face of painful or confusing interactions.

Creating a Balanced Narrative

The goal isn't to prove that your version of events is the absolute truth or to dismiss or erase your own understanding of your family history. Rather, the aim is to cultivate what therapists refer to as "narrative flexibility"—the capacity to hold your own truth with clarity and compassion while also remaining open to the perspectives and experiences of others.

Again, as emphasized previously, this doesn't mean abandoning your story or invalidating your feelings. Instead, it's about recognizing that multiple narratives can coexist, each shaped by different memories, emotions, and contexts. Developing this kind of mental and emotional flexibility can lead to greater empathy, improved relationships, and a deeper, more balanced understanding of the past.

Steps toward narrative flexibility:

1. Acknowledge your perspective is shaped by:

    - Your role as parent
    - Your generational context
    - Your cultural background
    - Your own childhood experiences

2. Recognize that your adult child's perspective is influenced by:

    - Their role as child
    - Their generational context
    - Their current life stage
    - Their emotional needs

3. Consider how both perspectives might contain truth:

    - Different roles create different experiences
    - Same events can have different impacts
    - Love and hurt can coexist
    - Good intentions don't always prevent pain

Sandra reflects:

> *"Understanding that my son could have a completely different*

experience of our family life without invalidating my memories was a turning point. I could hold onto the love I knew I gave while accepting that he might have needed or wanted something different—at least some of the time."

In this exploration we aren't trying to assign blame but about deepening understanding—of yourself, your adult child, and the complex dynamics that shape family relationships.

Their Story: Understanding Without Accepting

When Maria found her daughter's blog post detailing her "traumatic childhood," her first instinct was to dispute every point, to defend herself against what felt like character assassination. "I wanted to comment with photos of happy moments, to prove her wrong," she says. "But I realized that wouldn't help either of us. Instead, I tried to understand why she might see things so differently."

Understanding your adult child's narrative doesn't mean accepting blame or invalidating your experience. Rather, it's about developing what psychologists call "perspective flexibility"—the ability to consider different viewpoints while maintaining your emotional boundaries.

> **Questions for Perspective Exploration**
>
> When examining family narratives, consider:
>
> ❖ What was happening in the larger family context?
> ❖ What were the unspoken expectations?
> ❖ Were there needs that weren't being met?
> ❖ What cultural factors were at play?
> ❖ What generational patterns were operating?
> ❖ What was understood but never discussed?

Common Themes in Adult Children's Narratives

Dr. Joshua Coleman, in his work *Rules of Estrangement* (2020), notes several recurring themes in adult children's narratives:

- Feeling unseen or unheard.
- Experiencing emotional neglect despite material provision.

- Perceiving control rather than protection.
- Feeling responsible for parent's emotional well-being.
- Identifying impacts of unintentional harm.
- Struggling with unmet emotional needs.

Current Culture and Outside Influences

Our adult children are living in a world that talks openly about mental health, therapy, and family dynamics—more than any generation before them. With access to therapy, social media, and supportive peer groups, they're encouraged to look at their childhood in new ways. What they learn can sometimes feel very different from how their parents remember things.

Therapy can bring fresh insight or change how someone sees past events. Social media adds more voices—some helpful, others overwhelming—shaping how adult children understand their upbringing. Friends and online communities may offer support, but can also pressure them to view the past in a certain light.

> ### Understanding Without Self-Blame
>
> **Instead of:** "I must have been a terrible parent."
> **Consider:** "Different needs and perspectives existed."
>
> **Instead of:** "Everything I did was wrong."
> **Consider:** "Impact can differ from intention."
>
> **Instead of:** "I have to accept their version completely."
> **Consider:** "Multiple experiences can coexist."

Words like "generational trauma," "emotional invalidation," and "attachment issues" are now common in these conversations. These ideas help younger generations make sense of their emotions, but they can also lead to judgments about parenting that feel harsh or unfamiliar to parents who did their best with the tools they had.

Many estranged parents feel heartbroken, confused, and left behind. They may not understand the language their children now use or why things that once seemed normal are now seen as harmful. It's painful to feel misunderstood—especially when parenting was done with love and care.

Some families find their way back through open, honest conversations and a willingness to listen. Others stay separated, unsure how to move forward. But in every case, healing starts with empathy and curiosity—on both sides.

Today's world has changed how people think about families. That doesn't mean parents are to blame—but it does mean we all need new ways to understand each other if we want to rebuild trust and connection.

EXERCISE: Perspective Bridge

Consider a significant family event from your adult child's possible viewpoint:

1. What was their age and developmental stage?

   _____

2. What else was happening in their life?

   _____

   _____

3. What might they have needed that wasn't obvious?

   _____

   _____

4. How might they have interpreted your actions then and now?

   _____

   _____

> 5. What cultural messages were they receiving then or are receiving now about this event?
>
> _____
>
> _____
>
> _____
>
> Remember: This exercise isn't about self-blame but about expanding understanding.

A Word About Therapy:

For parents facing the painful reality of estrangement from their adult children, it's important to know that therapy doesn't always lead to reconciliation. While therapy can help adult children process emotions and gain insight, it can also sometimes encourage a more rigid view of family relationships.

Mental health professionals are increasingly aware that therapy—especially when it focuses on individual healing and boundary-setting—can sometimes lead adult children to see family dynamics in black-and-white terms. This might mean focusing mostly on past mistakes rather than the full picture of the relationship and the possibility of healing and growing it.

Some experts have raised concerns that certain therapeutic approaches may unintentionally encourage all-or-nothing thinking, where adult children come to believe that cutting off contact is the only healthy choice—even when that distance might be causing more harm than good.

This doesn't mean all therapy is bad. It means parents should understand that their child's perception of the healing process might not include reconnection. In today's culture, where individual well-being is heavily emphasized, it can be hard for adult children to balance self-care with understanding other viewpoints.

For parents who hope to rebuild the relationship, this situation calls for patience, self-reflection, and possibly their own therapeutic support to work through the emotional challenges of estrangement.

Maintaining Your Truth While Listening to Your Child

Robert shares:

> *"The hardest part was learning how to listen to my son's perspective without drowning in guilt or defending every action. I had to find middle ground between complete denial and total self-blame."*

Guidelines for Engaging with Different Narratives:

1. Set emotional boundaries

   - Recognize when you need to step back
   - Take breaks from difficult content
   - Maintain your self-care practices

2. Practice perspective-taking in small doses

   - Start with less triggering memories
   - Work with a counselor if needed
   - Journal about insights and reactions

3. Acknowledge without over-apologizing

   - "I hear that was your experience"
   - "I understand this impacted you differently"
   - "I'm sorry you felt that way"

4. Maintain your own truth while listening

   - "I had different intentions, but I hear your pain"
   - "My experience was different, but your feelings are valid"
   - "I can see how it looked from your perspective"

The True Story: Finding Middle Ground

As we navigate competing narratives, the goal isn't to determine a single "true" version of events, but to understand how different perspectives can coexist. Family truth is rarely simple, and family experiences reflect different lights depending on where you stand.

Consider Amanda's journey:

> *"For years, I insisted my version of events was the only accurate one. I had photos, videos, calendar entries—proof of happy times. But when I finally allowed myself to consider that my daughter might have experienced those same moments differently, something shifted. Not in our relationship, but in my understanding of how complex family memories can be."*

Moving Beyond Binary Thinking

The human mind naturally seeks certainty, making it challenging to hold seemingly contradictory truths. However, family relationships often exist in these gray areas where:

- Love and hurt can coexist
- Good intentions can have unintended impacts
- Happy memories can hold different meanings
- Protection can feel like control
- Provision can miss emotional needs

EXERCISE: Exploring Multiple Truths

Choose a significant family memory and consider:

- What this event meant to you at the time?

_____

_____

- What it might have meant to your adult child?

  _____
  _____

- What circumstances influenced each perspective?

  _____
  _____
  _____

- What needs were present for each person?

  _____
  _____
  _____

- How both experiences can be valid?

  _____
  _____
  _____

When parents can hold space for multiple truths without losing their own emotional ground, they often find greater peace—regardless of the current state of the relationship.

Creating Space for Understanding

Remember to keep in mind that finding middle ground doesn't mean abandoning your experience or accepting blame. Instead, it involves developing what therapists call "narrative flexibility"—the ability to:

- Consider different viewpoints without self-judgment
- Acknowledge impact without assuming intention
- Recognize how roles shaped perspectives
- Accept that memory serves different purposes
- Understand how present circumstances color past events

> **Signs of Growing Narrative Flexibility**
>
> You're developing narrative flexibility when you can:
>
> ❖ Listen to different perspectives without becoming defensive.
> ❖ Hold your truth while acknowledging others.
> ❖ Consider context rather than seeking absolute right/wrong.
> ❖ Recognize how roles influenced experiences.
> ❖ Accept that reconciling all viewpoints may not be possible.

This journey toward understanding requires patience, self-compassion, and often professional support. As you work to integrate different perspectives, remember that your goal is growth and healing, not perfect agreement or resolution.

Practical Tools for Navigating Different Narratives

Learning to hold multiple perspectives while maintaining your emotional equilibrium requires specific skills and practices. Think of it like developing a new muscle—it takes consistent, gentle exercise and a willingness to work through initial discomfort.

In my relationship with my daughter, taking her perspective into account—including her mental health challenges—helped me move past the hurt, anger, and helplessness, and instead see her as someone I deeply hoped would heal enough to find connection and happiness.

The Mirror Exercise

One powerful tool for exploring perspective involves using physical mirrors to symbolically represent different viewpoints. By positioning mirrors to reflect various angles of a subject, scene, or even oneself, artists and storytellers can visualize how perception shifts depending on where one stands—both literally and figuratively. This technique not only aids in developing spatial awareness and composition, but also serves as a metaphor for understanding conflicting perspectives or hidden truths within a narrative.

Linda describes her experience:

> *"My therapist had me set up three mirrors, representing my perspective, my daughter's perspective, and what she called 'the larger truth.' Looking into each one helped me understand how the same events could appear so different depending on where you stand."*

EXERCISE: Three Mirrors Reflection

Set up your space:

1. Find a quiet, private area.
2. Position three mirrors (or symbolic objects)
3. Label them: "My Truth," "Their Truth," "Larger Truth"
4. Choose a specific memory to explore

For each mirror, consider:

- What emotions arise?
- What needs were present?
- What fears or hopes existed?
- What remained unspoken?
- What understanding emerges?

Perspective exercises help parents develop a greater ability to hold complex, sometimes conflicting emotions and viewpoints at the same time, while staying emotionally steady. These practices encourage empathy, patience, and resilience, allowing parents to handle challenging situations with more clarity and calm. This, in turn, supports healthier and more thoughtful responses within the family.

Creating a Narrative Timeline

Understanding how different perspectives develop often involves examining the broader context of events. Creating a parallel timeline that shows both your experience and potential alternative viewpoints.

Thomas shares:

> *"When I mapped out my son's teenage years, I included what was happening in my life—the promotion at work, the cross-country move—alongside what he might have been experiencing. Seeing it laid out helped me understand how differently we might have interpreted those years."*

Safety Guidelines for Perspective Work

- ❖ Start with less triggering memories
- ❖ Have support resources ready
- ❖ Take breaks when needed
- ❖ Journal your insights
- ❖ Practice self-compassion
- ❖ Seek professional help if overwhelmed

EXERCISE: Parallel Timeline Creation

On your timeline, note:

Your Experience:

- Significant events
- Your emotional state

- Your intentions
- Your understanding at the time

Possible Alternative Experience:

- Impact on others
- Different interpretations
- Unspoken needs
- Cultural influences

Remember, this exercise aims to expand understanding rather than assign blame or responsibility.

As you develop these tools for holding multiple perspectives, remember that understanding different viewpoints doesn't require abandoning your own truth or accepting blame for every difficulty. Instead, it creates space for deeper understanding and potential healing—whether or not reconciliation occurs.

Communication Strategies for Narrative Work

Even when parents begin to understand that there are multiple ways to interpret past experiences, actually talking about those differences can be surprisingly difficult. Recognizing that more than one truth exists doesn't automatically lead to open or healing conversations.

Parents often struggle to share their own perspectives without sounding like they're dismissing their child's version of events—or

> **Questions for Timeline Exploration**
>
> For each significant event, consider:
> ❖ What pressures were you under?
> ❖ What was happening culturally?
> ❖ What remained unspoken?
> ❖ What needs weren't met?
> ❖ What assumptions were made?
> ❖ What support was available?

contradicting things they've said in the past. It's especially tricky to validate a child's emotional reality while also offering another way of seeing the situation. Timing matters, too; sharing an alternative view too soon can feel confusing or even threatening to an adult child who's still working through pain.

On top of that, the natural imbalance in the parent-child relationship can make any differing perspective feel like criticism. The challenge is finding a way to gently expand your child's understanding without making them feel unheard or unsafe. Doing this well takes not just insight, but emotional sensitivity and communication skills—many of which parents are still learning, often in parallel with their adult children.

Dr. Joshua Coleman advises:

> *"The goal in healing estrangement isn't to prove who's right, but to create understanding while maintaining emotional boundaries."*

Developing Communication Guidelines

For parents of estranged adult children, preparing emotionally and mentally before any future conversation is one of the most important things you can do. Take time to reflect on your own emotional triggers, defensive habits, and communication patterns—especially those that may have played a role in the estrangement. Think about what topics you're truly ready to discuss and which ones still feel too sensitive. Be honest with yourself about your goals: Are you hoping to better understand your child? To share your own feelings? To begin healing the relationship?

Writing down your thoughts in advance can help, but stay open and ready to truly listen. Approach the conversation with curiosity instead of a need to explain or defend. Be willing to hear hard truths—even if they're painful—without immediately reacting or justifying past choices.

Even if you're not in contact with your child right now, this preparation still matters. Estrangement can shift unexpectedly—your child might reach out during a major life change, a crisis, or simply when they're ready. If that moment comes, you'll be better prepared to respond calmly and thoughtfully rather than out of emotion.

Now is the time to focus on your own growth. That might mean working with a therapist, joining a support group, or learning more about communication and emotional regulation. Practice active listening. Explore different ways people express themselves. Reflect on your own role in the relationship's history.

Remember, this isn't about crafting the perfect argument to "win" your child back. It's about becoming the kind of parent who can meet a fragile moment with honesty, humility, and care. Even the smallest interactions—a short text, a quick call, or a chance meeting—can be meaningful if you're emotionally ready to meet them with grace and openness.

Before engaging in any discussion about differing perspectives, establish clear internal guidelines:

1. Focus on Understanding, Not Winning

   - Listen more than you speak
   - Ask questions rather than defend
   - Acknowledge feelings before facts
   - Stay curious about different viewpoints

2. Maintain Emotional Safety

   - Set clear boundaries
   - Take breaks when needed
   - Use "I" statements
   - Avoid absolutes (you always do this, I never feel that)

Productive vs. Unproductive Communication

Productive:

"I hear that you experienced that differently"

"Help me understand your perspective"

"That wasn't my intention, but I see the impact"

"I need time to process this"

Unproductive:

"That's not what happened"

"You're remembering it wrong"

"I did the best I could"

"You're being unfair"

3. Practice Self-Protection
   - Prepare support systems
   - Have grounding techniques ready
   - Know your triggers
   - Plan exit strategies

Dr. Karl Pillemer notes:

> *"Parents who develop the ability to consider multiple perspectives while maintaining their own emotional stability often achieve greater peace, regardless of reconciliation outcomes."*

EXERCISE: Communication Practice Scenarios

With a therapist or trusted friend, practice responding to challenging statements. For example:

Scenario 1: "You never supported my dreams."
Practice Response: "I want to understand how you came to feel that way. Would you share more?"

Scenario 2: "You were always controlling."
Practice Response: "I see now that my protection might have felt like control. Can you tell me more about your experience?"

When you're dealing with estrangement from an adult child, it's natural to experience a wide range of painful emotions—grief, confusion, anger, guilt, and sadness. One of the most important things you can do for yourself during this time is to build emotional resilience—the ability to stay grounded and steady, even when your heart feels broken.

As you try to understand different points of view or make sense of what led to the estrangement, remember to take care of your own emotional and physical well-being. This isn't just helpful—it's necessary. You can't pour from an empty cup.

Make time for self-care, whether that means setting boundaries with others, finding quiet time for yourself, staying active, eating well, or seeking out things that bring you peace and joy.

Navigating complex family situations can take time, and there may not be easy answers. But by caring for yourself and staying open to growth and healing, you give yourself the strength to face each day and whatever the future may hold.

Looking Forward: Integration and Growth

As you develop skills for holding multiple narratives, you may notice shifts in how you relate to your own story. This growth serves you regardless of whether reconciliation occurs.

Dr. Kylie Agllias observes:

> *"Parents often discover that exploring different perspectives enriches rather than diminishes their understanding of family relationships."*

Signs of Growing Perspective:

- Less defensive reactions to different viewpoints
- Increased comfort with complexity
- Better emotional regulation
- Clearer sense of personal boundaries
- Deeper self-compassion
- More nuanced understanding of relationships

As Maria reflects:

> *"Learning to hold different perspectives helped me find peace with my own story, even though my daughter's view remains very different. I've learned that understanding doesn't always mean agreement, and that's okay."*

Moving Forward with Multiple Truths

As we conclude this exploration of different narratives, it's important to remember that understanding multiple perspectives doesn't require:

- Abandoning your own truth
- Accepting all blame
- Dismissing your good intentions
- Invalidating your love and effort
- Denying your positive memories

This means that gaining perspective doesn't mean you surrender your story to someone else's version of events. You are simply making space to explore multiple perspectives without losing your own. When it comes to family dynamics, this approach allows for a more layered and compassionate understanding of how relationships form, fracture, and evolve. By acknowledging different narratives, you can uncover hidden patterns or unmet needs without dismissing your own experiences. The goal is clarity, not blame—and emotional resilience, not erasure. Through this process, you gain the freedom to shape your story with intention, honoring both truth and healing.

Patricia shares how she applies narrative flexibility in her daily life:

> "When I look at old family photos now, I can acknowledge both my joyful memories and the possibility that my daughter experienced those moments differently. This doesn't diminish my truth—it adds depth to my understanding."

As you continue developing narrative flexibility, remember that this work serves your healing regardless of the current state of your relationship with your adult child. In our next chapter, we'll explore specific writing techniques that can help

> **Questions for Building Perspective**
>
> When engaging with family memories or current situations, consider:
>
> ❖ What other perspectives might exist?
> ❖ What needs might have been present?
> ❖ How might roles have influenced experience?
> ❖ What remained unspoken?
> ❖ What assumptions am I making?

you process different narratives and emotions while strengthening your self-understanding and resilience.

National Crisis Hotline

If you're experiencing thoughts of self-harm or feeling overwhelmed call:

988
or
1-800-273-8255

Available 24/7 for support and guidance.

Remember: Taking breaks from this work is healthy and necessary.

CHAPTER 4:

The Power of the Pen— Journaling for Discovery and Release

SARAH SITS AT HER KITCHEN TABLE well past midnight, torn journal pages scattered around her like fallen leaves. For months, she's filled notebooks with angry letters she'll never send, pouring out her pain in harsh words and accusations. But tonight, something shifts as she reads an entry from six months ago. Between the lines of hurt and confusion, she finds an unexpected moment of grace—a small paragraph where she wrote about forgiving herself for being an imperfect mother.

"I never noticed that before," she whispers, touching the words gently. "I was so focused on the anger, I missed this moment of compassion."

If you've been hesitant to start journaling about your estrangement, you're not alone. Many parents worry that writing about their pain will only intensify it. Others fear confronting the complex emotions that estrangement brings up. Some simply don't know where to begin.

Writing about difficult experiences can feel daunting at first, especially when emotions are raw or unresolved. Yet research consistently shows that structured journaling—writing with intention and reflection—can be a powerful tool for emotional healing. It allows you to process grief, make sense of painful events, and reduce anxiety by giving form to feelings that might otherwise stay tangled or suppressed. Even when reconciliation with others isn't possible, the act of putting your story into words can offer clarity, release, and a renewed sense of inner strength.

Dr. James Pennebaker explains:

> "Expressive writing about emotional experiences can feel intimidating initially, but research consistently shows it can reduce distress and promote psychological well-being."

Understanding the Power of Therapeutic Writing

When we write about our experiences, something remarkable happens in our brains. The act of putting emotions into words helps move experiences from the emotional centers of the brain to areas associated with understanding and meaning. This shift alone can begin to reduce emotional intensity.

If you've completed the Grief Expression Letter from Chapter 1 or the Compassionate Observer Letter from Chapter 2, you've likely already felt the profound impact writing can have on your emotional and physical well-being.

When I wrote *Abandoned Mother*, my first book on estrangement that explored both my own journey and the experiences of other parents, I discovered a sense of peace that neither reading nor talking had been able to provide.

Research has demonstrated that regular therapeutic writing can:

- Lower stress hormones
- Improve immune function
- Reduce intrusive thoughts
- Increase emotional awareness

> **The Science Behind Therapeutic Writing**
>
> Research highlights:
>
> ❖ Twenty minutes of expressive writing can reduce physical stress markers.
>
> ❖ Regular journaling may improve immune system functioning.
>
> ❖ Writing about emotions activates different brain regions than just thinking about them.
>
> ❖ Structured writing exercises can help organize traumatic memories.

- Help process complex grief
- Build resilience

Maria discovered this power firsthand:

> "At first, I could barely write a sentence without crying. But gradually, putting my feelings on paper helped me see patterns in my emotions. I started to understand my grief differently. The pain didn't disappear, but it became more manageable."

Creating Your Safe Writing Space

Before diving into specific techniques, it's essential to establish a secure, private space for your writing practice. This isn't just about physical space—it's about creating emotional safety for vulnerable expression.

Dr. Kate Thompson notes:

> "Creating a safe, contained space for therapeutic writing is essential for allowing vulnerable self-expression."

Think of your writing space as a container for your emotions. It should feel private, comfortable, and free from judgment. This might be a physical corner of your home, or simply a special notebook that you keep secure.

EXERCISE: Setting Up Your Writing Space

Consider these elements:

Physical Space

- A quiet location where you won't be interrupted
- Comfortable seating
- Good lighting
- Privacy from others

Writing Tools

- A journal that feels inviting (or a laptop if you're tech-savvy)
- Pens that write smoothly
- Any meaningful objects that help you feel grounded
- Optional: tissues, comfort items, or objects to use as grounding tools

Emotional Safety

- Permission to write without censoring
- Agreement with yourself about privacy
- Plan for securing your writings
- Support resources readily available

Getting Started with Journaling

Many parents feel uncertain about how to begin their writing practice. Start where you are. There's no wrong way to begin—what matters is taking that first step, even if it's just writing "I don't know what to write."

Dr. Louise DeSalvo emphasizes:

> *"Writing about positive experiences and gratitude, even during difficult times, can help build resilience and emotional balance."*

Basic Journaling Techniques

Free Writing

Begin with simple, unstructured writing. Set a timer for 5-10 minutes and write whatever comes to mind without editing or judging. This helps bypass your internal critic and access deeper emotions.

Sarah shares:

> *"I started by just writing 'I miss my daughter' over and over.*

> *It felt mechanical at first, but eventually, other thoughts and feelings started flowing."*

Structured Prompts

If free writing feels overwhelming, try responding to specific prompts:

- Today I'm feeling . . .
- What I wish I could say . . .
- One thing I need right now . . .
- A memory that brings me peace . . .

Time-Limited Writing

Start with short writing sessions—even just five minutes. This helps prevent emotional flooding and builds confidence in the process.

Dr. Kate Thompson, a journal therapy specialist, advises:

> **Signs You Need a Break from Writing**
>
> ❖ Physical tension or distress
> ❖ Racing thoughts
> ❖ Emotional overwhelm
> ❖ Difficulty focusing
> ❖ Strong urge to destroy what you've written
>
> Remember: You can always pause and return later.

> *"Short writing sessions of five to ten minutes can help build confidence while preventing emotional overwhelm."*

Overcoming Common Challenges

Some parents worry that they don't have writing skills, but writing for healing doesn't require literary greatness or even correct spelling. The focus is on expressing emotions and processing experiences. Your only audience is yourself.

Dr. James Pennebaker explains:

> *"The goal isn't to create great literature but to use writing as a tool for understanding and healing."*

Another common concern is the reluctance to dwell on painful thoughts. But writing about experiences often has the opposite effect, helping you to release the repetitive thoughts that can be so damaging.

Jennifer tells about her challenge:

> *"I worried writing about my pain and anger would make everything worse. But my therapist helped me understand that acknowledging feelings isn't the same as dwelling on them. Writing actually helps me move through emotions rather than getting stuck in them."*

The worry that someone else will read it is another major block to writing. It's true that some emotions you may not want to share with anyone.

Consider these privacy strategies:

- Keep your journal in a secure location
- Use a password-protected digital journal
- Destroy pages after writing if needed
- Create a code system for sensitive content

EXERCISE: Starting Small

Choose one of these brief writing prompts:

- List three emotions you're experiencing right now.
- Write two sentences about your hopes.
- Describe a moment of strength.
- Express one wish for your future.

Spend just 3-5 minutes with your chosen prompt. Notice how it feels to put these thoughts on paper.

Building a Writing Habit

The most effective journaling practice is the one you can sustain consistently over time. Whether it's a quick five-minute reflection each morning or a deeper, more involved session once a week, the key is finding a rhythm that fits naturally into your life. Consistency builds momentum, allowing your thoughts to unfold gradually and your self-awareness to deepen. It's not about how much you write, but about showing up regularly, creating a space where your mind can speak and be heard.

Dr. Louise DeSalvo notes:

> *"The most beneficial writing practice is one that can be maintained regularly, even if brief."*

In creating your writing ritual, consider these elements:

1. Time:
   - Choose a consistent time
   - Set realistic expectations
   - Start small and build gradually

2. Environment:
   - Find a private space
   - Minimize distractions
   - Create comfortable surroundings

3. Preparation:
   - Gather your materials
   - Take a few centering breaths
   - Set an intention for your writing

Digital vs. Paper Journaling

Digital Benefits:
- Password protection
- Easy editing
- Searchable entries
- Accessible anywhere

Paper Benefits:
- More intimate connection
- No screen fatigue
- Fewer distractions
- Therapeutic hand-brain connection

Choose what feels most comfortable and secure for you.

Moving Beyond Basic Writing

As you become more comfortable with regular journaling, you might want to explore more structured approaches.

Think of it has a tool in your healing journey. You can try different approaches depending on your emotional needs on any given day.

Dr. Stephen Lepore emphasizes:

> *"Writing about difficult emotions and hidden aspects of our experience can reduce their power over us."*

Structured Writing Exercises

Unsent Letters

One of the most powerful therapeutic writing tools is the unsent letter. These letters allow you to express feelings and thoughts that might be too raw or complex for direct communication. These don't necessarily have to be to your estranged child but can also be to yourself, other family members, or even grandchildren. Unsent letters provide a safe place to hold difficult emotions. You can be completely honest without worrying about the impact on others or managing their responses.

Types of Unsent Letters:

- Letters to your estranged adult child
- Letters to your younger self
- Letters from your future self
- Letters to your pain or grief
- Letters to your anger or shame

EXERCISE: Writing Your First Unsent Letter

Choose one of these prompts:

"Dear [Name], What I wish you knew . . ."

"Dear Younger Me, About this journey . . ."

"Dear Future Self, I need you to know . . ."

Guidelines:

- Write without censoring.
- Include both feelings and facts.
- Express needs and wishes.
- Allow for complexity.
- Close with self-compassion.

Patricia shares:

> *"Writing letters to my son helped me express things I couldn't say out loud. Eventually, I started writing letters to myself too, and that's when real healing began."*

Dialogue Writing

This technique involves creating written conversations between different parts of yourself or with others in your life. Dialogue writing can help reveal new perspectives and unlock emotional insights we might miss through regular journaling.

Dr. James Pennebaker observes:

> *"Writing about shame with self-awareness can help separate our worth from our pain."*

EXERCISE: Inner Dialogue Template

Create a conversation between:

- Your heart and your head
- Your grief and your hope
- Your past and present self
- Your fear and your wisdom
- Your anger and your compassion

Example Format:

Heart: I miss her so much it physically hurts.
Head: I understand. But remember how far we've come.
Heart: Some days it feels impossible to go on.
Head: Yet here we are, still moving forward . . .

_____

_____

_____

Timeline Exploration

Creating a written timeline can help you process events and identify patterns without becoming overwhelmed by emotions. Start with significant moments, both positive and challenging. Look for turning points, patterns, and places where you might discover new understanding.

Future Self Work

Writing from or to your future self can help create hope and perspective. This technique helps you envision possibilities beyond current pain while acknowledging your present experience. Writing to yourself builds a bridge between current struggles and potential healing. It reminds us that while pain is real, it isn't permanent.

Timeline Writing Guidelines

Include:
- Key events
- Emotional milestones
- Changes in relationships
- Your responses
- Lessons learned
- Moments of growth

Remember:
- Focus on facts first
- Add emotions later
- Notice patterns
- Include positive moments
- Mark points of resilience

EXERCISE: Future Self Letter

Imagine yourself three years from now, writing back to your present self. Consider:

- What healing has occurred?
- What wisdom have you gained?
- What would you want your present self to know?
- What compassion would you offer?
- What hope would you share?

Tips for Future Self Writing:

- Be realistically optimistic.
- Acknowledge both growth and ongoing challenges.

- Include specific details.
- Express compassion for present struggles.
- Share concrete wisdom.

Michael reflects:

> *"Writing from my future self helped me see that my identity wasn't limited to being an estranged parent. I could imagine a life that held both this pain and new possibilities."*

Gratitude Practice

Gratitude writing can feel especially difficult during times of estrangement. For me, it was one of the hardest practices to adopt. I eventually realized why: I didn't *want* to see anything good. I wanted to stay in my pain—a pain that, in a strange way, felt addictive. But when I began to consistently notice the good in my life, something shifted. I started to understand that I could hold both truths at once: the hurt and the hope.

Writing about gratitude is a powerful tool for building emotional resilience. It doesn't deny the existence of pain—it makes room for the possibility that good things can exist alongside difficult experiences.

> ### When Future Writing Feels Hard
>
> If imagining the future feels overwhelming:
>
> ❖ Start with smaller time frames.
> ❖ Focus on inner rather than external changes.
> ❖ Write about hope without requiring specific outcomes.
> ❖ Include current strengths that will help you move forward.
> ❖ Remember that healing doesn't require reconciliation.

EXERCISE: Gratitude Writing Framework

Start with small, concrete observations:

- One moment of peace today
- A kind gesture from someone
- A physical comfort you experienced
- Something beautiful you noticed
- A small accomplishment

_____

_____

_____

Linda shares:

> *"At first, writing about gratitude felt impossible—even offensive. How could I be grateful when my heart was broken? But my therapist suggested starting with tiny things: my morning coffee, a warm shower, my cat's purr. Gradually, I found I could hold both grief and gratitude."*

Writing Through Different Emotional States

Every parent experiencing estrangement cycles through various emotional states. Your writing practice can adapt to wherever you are emotionally. Even different writing techniques serve different emotional needs. Learning to match your writing approach with your current experience can make your journaling more effective and habitual.

Dr. Kate Thompson explains:

> *"Different writing approaches serve different emotional needs. Learning to match technique to current state enhances effectiveness."*

Writing Through Anger

Anger is a natural and valid response to estrangement. "Many parents feel guilty about their anger, but this emotion often masks deeper feelings of hurt and powerlessness. Writing can help us express anger safely while accessing these underlying emotions.

Safety Notes for Anger Writing

- ❖ Keep writing private.
- ❖ Focus on feelings, not actions.
- ❖ Avoid making threats.
- ❖ Consider destroying pages afterward.
- ❖ Have support resources ready.

> **EXERCISE: Anger Release Writing**
>
> 1. Choose your method:
>   - Fast, aggressive writing
>   - List-making
>   - Stream of consciousness
>   - Physical release (tear or crumple pages)
> 2. Set a time limit (5-15 minutes)
> 3. Write without censorship about:
>   - What makes you angry
>   - Why it's unfair
>   - What you wish you could say
>   - How your body feels
>   - What you need right now
> 4. Close with a grounding practice:
>   - Deep breathing
>   - Physical movement
>   - Comfort activity
>   - Self-compassion statement

Writing Through Grief

Grief in estrangement can be particularly complex because it involves mourning someone who is still alive. As I mentioned earlier, the vastness of this grief—layered with pain, anger, and longing—can become strangely addictive, almost woven into our identity.

Writing can provide a way to gently untangle those threads. It offers a private space to explore the contradictions of love and loss, to express what feels unspeakable, and to begin releasing what no longer serves us. Through writing, we don't erase the grief—we make room to understand it, to witness it, and, eventually, to move through it.

Patricia shares:

> "Some days, my journal is just filled with 'I miss you' written over and over. Other days, I can write about memories or hopes. Both kinds of entries help me process this strange grief."

EXERCISE: Gentle Grief Writing

When grief feels overwhelming:

1. Start with simple statements

   - "Today I miss . . ."
   - "I remember when . . ."
   - "My heart feels . . ."
   - "I wish . . ."
   - "I hope . . ."

2. Allow space for

   - Memories
   - Current feelings
   - Future wishes
   - Unanswered questions
   - Small comforts

3. Close with self-care

   - Gratitude note
   - Comfort memory
   - Self-compassion statement
   - Future hope
   - Present moment anchor

As with other exercises, grief writing doesn't need to be lengthy or profound.

Dr. Louise DeSalvo notes:

> *"Grief writing need not be elaborate—simply acknowledging our pain on paper can bring relief."*

Writing Through Shame

As we explored in Chapter 2, a strong sense of shame usually accompanies estrangement. Writing can help transform shame into self-compassion.

Dr. James Pennebaker observes:

> *"Writing about shame with self-awareness can help separate our worth from our pain."*

EXERCISE: Shame-to-Compassion Writing

1. Identify the shame statement:

   Example: "I must be a terrible mother for this to happen."

   _____

2. Question the statement:

   - Where did this belief come from?
   - What evidence supports or challenges it?
   - How would I respond to a friend saying this?
   - What would my wisest self say?

   _____

   _____

   _____

   _____

3. Write a compassionate response:

    - Acknowledge the pain
    - Challenge the shame
    - Offer understanding
    - Include hope
    - Express self-care

    _____

    _____

    _____

    _____

    _____

    _____

    _____

Sarah reflects:

> "Writing helped me see how harsh I was being with myself. Gradually, I learned to respond to my shame with the same kindness I'd show a friend going through this."

Exploring Forgiveness Through Writing

Many parents feel pressured to forgive quickly, even when the estrangement remains unresolved. Writing can offer a way to explore forgiveness at your own pace, honoring both your openness and your hesitation. Whether you're considering forgiveness for yourself, your adult child, or others involved in the estrangement, it's often a complex and nonlinear journey. Writing about forgiveness doesn't mean pushing yourself to feel something before you're ready—it means gently exploring what forgiveness could look like for you wherever you are in this journey.

Dr. Stephen Lepore explains:

> *"Writing about forgiveness allows us to explore its meaning at our own pace."*

Signs Writing Is Helping

- Decreased intensity of painful emotions
- More self-compassionate inner dialogue
- Better ability to express feelings
- Clearer perspective on situations
- Increased emotional resilience
- Growing sense of possibility

EXERCISE: Forgiveness Exploration Writing

Begin by considering these questions:

- What does forgiveness mean to me?

  _____

  _____

- What would forgiveness make possible?

  _____

  _____

- What stands in the way of forgiveness?

  _____

  _____

- What am I ready to release?

  _____

  _____

- What do I need to hold onto for now?

  _____

  _____

Building Self-Compassion Through Writing

Self-compassion writing builds on the work we've done with shame transformation, creating a foundation for sustainable emotional healing.

Dr. Gillie Bolton emphasizes:

> *"Regular writing practice can help develop self-compassion and transform our inner dialogue."*

Types of Forgiveness Writing

- Forgiveness letters (unsent)
- Forgiveness dialogues
- Release ceremonies through writing
- Future-self forgiveness vision
- Small steps toward acceptance

Remember: Forgiveness is a personal journey, not a requirement for healing. Be gentle with yourself.

> **EXERCISE: Daily Self-Compassion Check-In**
>
> **Morning Writing:**
>
> - One thing I appreciate about myself
> - A kind wish for my day
> - A reminder of my strength
>
> **Evening Writing:**
>
> - A moment of self-kindness today
> - Something I handled well
> - A gentle truth I'm learning

Patricia shares:

> *"Writing to myself with compassion felt awkward at first—even fake. But over time, it became more natural. Now it's like having a conversation with a wise, loving friend who happens to be me."*

Creating New Narratives

The final stage of therapeutic writing involves crafting new narratives that honor both your pain and your potential. Rather than denying the reality of estrangement, it focuses on expanding your story beyond it.

Begin to see yourself not only as the main character in your life's unfolding story but also as its author—the one who shapes the narrative moving forward. As you reflect, consider: What themes are rising to the surface besides loss? Are there threads of resilience, healing, or transformation? What inner strengths are coming into focus—courage, clarity, compassion? And as the pages turn, what new chapters might you write for yourself—chapters filled with meaning, connection, or renewed purpose?

Dr. Kate Thompson suggests:

> *"We can use writing to explore new ways of understanding our story beyond loss."*

EXERCISE: New Narrative Development

1. Current Chapter:

   - Where am I now in my story?

   _____

   _____

   - What themes are present?

   _____

   _____

   - What strengths am I showing?

   _____

   _____

2. Emerging Possibilities:

   - What new roles am I developing?

   _____

   _____

- What interests am I discovering?

  _____

  _____

- What connections am I building?

  _____

  _____

  _____

3. Future Chapters:

   - What possibilities exist beyond pain?

     _____

     _____

   - What wisdom am I gaining?

     _____

     _____

   - What legacy am I creating?

     _____

     _____

     _____

Your story continues beyond estrangement, and you hold the pen. Only you have the power to rewrite your narrative, change your direction, and transform your reactions to circumstances beyond your control. This isn't about hoping your child will change or waiting for reconciliation—this is about recognizing that you can reshape your entire experience starting today.

Consider someone who loses a career they've devoted decades to building—not through any fault of their own, but due to forces completely outside their control. Initially, their story revolves around loss, anger, and feeling powerless. But the moment they decide to take action—researching new paths, confronting difficult truths about themselves, actively pursuing change—everything shifts. They discover resilience they didn't know they possessed, creativity that had been dormant, and possibilities they'd never considered. What began as a story of endings transforms into one of new beginnings, but only because they chose to become the active force in their own narrative.

> **Elements of a Healing Narrative**
>
> ❖ Acknowledges both pain and growth.
> ❖ Includes multiple roles and identities.
> ❖ Recognizes ongoing evolution.
> ❖ Holds space for hope.
> ❖ Honors personal resilience.
> ❖ Allows for uncertainty.

The same transformative power exists for you as a parent facing estrangement. You cannot control your child's choices, but you have complete authority over how you respond, grow, and move forward. The question isn't whether change is possible—it's whether you're ready to claim your power to create it. Therapeutic writing helps you begin moving in the right direction.

The Role of Regular Review

Reviewing your journal entries over time can provide valuable insights into your healing journey. Set aside time monthly to read past entries. Look for patterns, progress, and recurring themes. This practice can help you recognize growth that might otherwise go unnoticed.

Dr. James Pennebaker suggests:

> "Regular review of our writing helps us recognize patterns and track our progress over time."

EXERCISE: Monthly Journal Review

Consider these questions:

- What themes do you notice?
- How have your emotions evolved?
- What insights keep emerging?
- Where do you see progress?
- What needs more attention?
- What new understanding has developed?

Remember: Focus on noticing patterns rather than judging content. Every entry represents a step in your healing journey.

Writing Your Way Forward

As we conclude our exploration of therapeutic writing, remember that your journal is more than just a collection of words—it's a witness to your journey, a container for your emotions, and a tool for discovering your own wisdom.

Sarah, whom we met at the beginning of this chapter, reflects:

> "My journal became my most trusted confidant. Through writing, I found parts of myself I thought I'd lost in the pain of estrangement."

Key Takeaways:

- Writing provides a safe space to express difficult emotions.
- Start small and build gradually.
- Different writing techniques serve different healing needs.
- Regular practice builds emotional resilience.
- Your journal is yours alone—there are no "rules."
- Progress happens gradually through consistent engagement.
- Writing can reveal insights that thinking alone cannot.
- Review periodically for insights.

In our next chapter, we'll explore how to use the insights gained through writing to shift our perspective on past events and current challenges. We'll learn specific techniques for reframing difficult situations while maintaining emotional boundaries and self-compassion. The writing skills you've developed here will serve as valuable tools as we work on transforming how we view our journey through estrangement.

National Crisis Hotline

If you're experiencing thoughts of self-harm or feeling overwhelmed call:

988

or

1-800-273-8255

Available 24/7 for support and guidance.

Remember: You can always pause, take a break, or seek support when needed. Your emotional safety comes first.

CHAPTER 5:

Reframing Your Lens—Shifting from Blame to Understanding

Margaret stands in her kitchen, holding a Mother's Day card from five years ago—the last one she received before her daughter stopped speaking to her. The familiar wave of shame rises: "I must have been a terrible mother." But today, something shifts. She pauses, takes a deep breath, and tries a new thought: "This situation is complex, and while I made mistakes, I also loved deeply."

This small moment represents a profound shift in thinking—one that's essential for healing from estrangement. As we explored in Chapter 4, writing can help us process our emotions and experiences. Now, we'll focus on how to consciously reshape our thoughts about estrangement, moving from self-blame to deeper understanding.

Parents often get stuck in patterns of black-and-white thinking about estrangement. The truth usually lies somewhere in between, but it takes certain thinking skills to see that middle ground.

Dr. Joshua Coleman notes:

> "Parents often vacillate between seeing themselves as terrible parents who deserve to be cut off and seeing their children as cruel and ungrateful. Neither position is helpful nor typically accurate."

Understanding Cognitive Reframing

Cognitive reframing means changing the way we think about a situation. It doesn't mean ignoring pain or pretending everything's fine. Instead, it helps us see things more clearly and with more balance. When we're hurting, our thinking can become narrow and extreme, leading to rigid or all-or-nothing conclusions. Reframing helps us stay flexible and grounded, even when emotions are strong.

Research shows that parents who develop cognitive flexibility tend to:

- Experience less depression and anxiety.
- Maintain better self-care practices.
- Navigate social situations more comfortably.
- Respond to triggers more effectively.
- Build stronger support networks.

> **What Reframing Is and Isn't**
>
> **Is:**
> - ❖ Seeing situations from multiple perspectives.
> - ❖ Acknowledging complexity.
> - ❖ Finding balanced truth.
> - ❖ Maintaining self-compassion.
>
> **Isn't:**
> - ❖ Denying pain or difficulty.
> - ❖ Forcing positive thinking.
> - ❖ Accepting all blame.
> - ❖ Dismissing valid feelings.

Patricia discovered this distinction through her healing journey:

> "At first, I thought reframing meant I had to pretend everything was fine or that the estrangement was somehow good for me. My therapist helped me understand that real reframing is about finding more helpful ways to understand my situation without denying its difficulty."

The Impact of Thought Patterns

How we think about estrangement deeply affects our emotions and healing. The stories we tell ourselves can trap us in shame and pain or help us heal and grow. These thoughts aren't just ideas—they shape how we feel, what we do, and whether we stay stuck or find the strength to move forward. Seeing the situation more realistically tends to help parents feel less depressed and become stronger over time.

Common Unhelpful Thought Patterns:

1. All-or-nothing thinking

    "I must have been a completely terrible parent."

2. Overgeneralization

    "Everything I did was wrong."

3. Mental filtering

    "None of the good times matter now."

4. Catastrophizing

    "I'll never be happy again."

5. Emotional reasoning

    "I feel like a failure, so I must be one."

EXERCISE: Identifying Your Thought Patterns

Take a moment to notice your typical thoughts about:

- Your role as a parent

    _____

    _____

    _____

- The estrangement itself

  _____

  _____

- Your adult child's decisions

  _____

  _____

- Your current situation

  _____

  _____

- Your future possibilities

  _____

  _____

Write down these thoughts without judgment. We'll work on reframing them as we continue.

Recognizing our own thought patterns is a crucial step toward personal growth. When we become aware of how we think and react, we open the door to change. This self-awareness allows us to step back, evaluate our perspective, and consciously decide how we want to respond, rather than being driven by automatic habits or assumptions.

The Impact of Social Judgment

As we discussed in Chapter 1, one of the hardest parts of estrangement is dealing with social situations and other people's judgments. These outside pressures can quietly shape the way we think and often reinforce negative thought patterns. In the next sections, we'll look at how social judgment affects our mindset and offer practical tools to help manage it.

Society often promotes unrealistic ideas about how parent-child relationships *should* look. So when a relationship breaks down, it can feel like a personal failure. Parents may carry heavy feelings of guilt and inadequacy, especially when they feel pressured to seem like perfect caregivers. These emotional burdens can cloud their thinking and strengthen harmful beliefs about their worth.

> **Common Social Scenarios and Reframing Options**
>
> **Instead of:** "Everyone must think I'm a terrible parent."
> **Try:** "Other people's opinions reflect their own fears and limited understanding."
>
> **Instead of:** "I have to explain everything."
> **Try:** "I can choose what to share based on my comfort level."
>
> **Instead of:** "I don't belong here anymore."
> **Try:** "I'm learning to navigate social spaces in new ways."

Social pressures around estrangement can show up in many ways. Holiday gatherings often highlight family relationships, making absence or tension more noticeable. Social media can add to the pressure by showing carefully curated images of "perfect" families. Friends may ask well-meaning but painful questions, not realizing how complicated the situation is. Cultural expectations about staying close as a family, along with religious or community judgments, can also weigh heavily. On top of that, there are often unspoken assumptions that parents are always at fault when a relationship breaks down.

EXERCISE: Identifying Social Triggers

List situations where social pressure intensifies your self-blame. Next to each trigger, note your typical thought response:

- Specific events (holidays, celebrations)

  _____

  _____

  _____

- Certain locations (family gathering spots)

  _____

  _____

  _____

  _____

- Particular people or groups

  _____

  _____

  _____

  _____

- Social media encounters

  _____

  _____

  _____

- Community activities

_____

_____

_____

_____

Creating New Thought Patterns

Changing how we think about our situation—especially in the face of social judgment—isn't just about staying positive. It's about seeing things more clearly. We need to build new ways of thinking that recognize both the pain of estrangement *and* our ability to grow and heal.

The first step in reframing is simply to notice the thought—become aware of when you're engaging in negative self-talk or all-or-nothing thinking. Once you've noticed it, pause. Give yourself a moment of space before reacting. Then, question the thought: Is this helping or hurting me? What evidence supports or challenges it? How would I see this if it were happening to a friend? Finally, choose a more balanced perspective—one that recognizes the situation's complexity rather than reducing it to extremes.

Patricia shares her experience:

> *"When my son didn't call on my birthday, my immediate thought was 'He must hate me completely.' Using the reframing steps, I paused and considered: 'This situation is painful AND complex. His feelings might be complicated, just as mine are.'"*

> **EXERCISE: Practice Basic Reframing**
>
> Choose a recent challenging thought about your estrangement:
>
> **Original Thought:** "I'm a complete failure as a parent."
>
> **Step 1 Notice:**
> Recognize this as all-or-nothing thinking.
>
> **Step 2 Pause:**
> Take three deep breaths.
>
> **Step 3 Question:**
>
> - Is this completely true?
> - What evidence exists for and against?
> - How would I counsel a friend thinking this?
>
> **Step 4 Choose:**
> "Parenting involves both successes and struggles. The current situation is painful but doesn't define my entire parenting journey."

At first, learning to shift our perspective may feel awkward or forced, like following a script. But over time, with consistent effort, the process becomes more intuitive. What once required deliberate steps can eventually happen quickly and naturally, often in the moment we need it most.

Identity Reframing

Parental estrangement shakes the foundation of who we are. For most, being a parent isn't just a role—it's part of their identity. The daily care, the purpose in raising a child, and hopes for their future become central to how parents see themselves. When a child distances themselves, parents often ask: "If I'm not actively parenting, am I still a parent?"

This can cause a deep sense of loss. Parents might feel all their efforts and sacrifices were for nothing. The challenge isn't to give up being a parent or ignoring the pain but to change how we see ourselves.

EXERCISE: Identity Expansion

List your roles and qualities beyond "parent":

- Personal characteristics
- Professional roles
- Other relationships
- Interests and passions
- Values and beliefs
- Life experiences

Melinda shares:

> "Being a parent was the center of my world—the daily care, the dreams I had for my child, it all defined me. When she cut off conversation, it felt like losing a part of myself. But over time, I've remembered that I was a person in my own right, with talents, goals, and dreams."

Reframing your identity after estrangement is a difficult but essential step toward healing. By recognizing the many parts that make you who you are—beyond just being a parent—you open the door to rediscovering your purpose and finding strength in your whole self. This broader view doesn't erase the pain, but it helps you carry it with resilience and hope.

Temporal Reframing

Temporal reframing is a technique that helps you view your current situation from different points in time—past, present, or future. By stepping outside the moment, you can gain a clearer, more balanced perspective. For example, looking back may help you see how far you've come, while imagining your future self can remind you that this pain won't last forever. Shifting your time perspective in this way can reduce emotional intensity and help you respond with greater clarity and self-compassion.

When we're hurting, everything feels permanent. A bad day feels like proof our whole life is ruined. A fight with someone feels like the relationship is over forever. Our pain tricks us into thinking the current moment will last forever. Taking a step back and thinking about time differently can help. The intense feelings and tough situations you're dealing with right now are temporary—they're just one part of your bigger life story, not the whole thing.

> **Temporal Reframing Examples**
>
> **Instead of:** "This pain will never end."
> **Try:** "This is a difficult chapter in a longer story."
>
> **Instead of:** "Everything is ruined forever."
> **Try:** "Right now is challenging, but life continues to unfold."
>
> **Instead of:** "I'll always be defined by this."
> **Try:** "This experience is part of my journey, not my whole story."

Dr. Karl Pillemer observes:

> *"The acute pain of estrangement can make it feel permanent and unchangeable. Yet research shows that many family rifts do heal over time, especially when parents maintain hope while respecting boundaries."*

To clarify temporal reframing, let's take a look at this analogy: When Marcus was passed over for a promotion he'd worked toward for months, his immediate reaction was devastating: "I'm clearly not good enough," he thought. "My career is going nowhere, and I'll never advance here." The rejection felt like proof of his inadequacy, and he considered quitting altogether.

But then Marcus looked backward and remembered that just two years ago, he'd been in an entry-level position, anxious about whether he even belonged in his field. Now he was being considered for senior roles—clear evidence of growth. Then he projected forward: "How will I view this moment five years from now?" He realized his future self would likely see this as a temporary setback, maybe even a redirect toward something better.

This shift in time perspective didn't erase his current disappointment, but it transformed his thoughts of a devastating verdict into a single data point in a longer story. Within weeks, Marcus felt motivated to seek feedback, develop new skills, and explore other opportunities—responses that his "in-the-moment" despair would never have allowed.

Naturally, losing a child is a far more severe life event than losing a job, but the principle of temporal reframing still applies. It doesn't diminish the grief, but it can offer a broader context over time: a shift from feeling permanently broken to gradually recognizing resilience, agency, and the possibility of meaning beyond the pain.

This doesn't make your current pain less real or important. But it helps you see it as one chapter instead of the entire book. Try asking yourself: "How will I probably see this situation in five years?" or "What would I tell a friend going through the same thing?" This bigger picture view naturally makes present difficulties feel less overwhelming while keeping you hopeful that things can get better.

EXERCISE: Time Perspective Shift

Consider your situation:

- How might you view this in five years?
- What wisdom might your future self offer?
- How does past experience inform current challenges?
- What possibilities exist beyond this moment?

Emotional Reframing: Working with Difficult Feelings

One of the hardest parts of estrangement is coping with the emotional intensity it brings. Overwhelming feelings can distort our thoughts, making them harsher and more self-critical. Emotional reframing offers a way to validate what we're feeling while also keeping a clearer, more compassionate view of ourselves and the situation.

Common emotional cycles in estrangement often follow predictable patterns:

- Trigger event occurs (holiday, birthday, social media post).
- Intense emotions arise (grief, shame, anger).
- Negative thought patterns activate.
- Behavior becomes reactive.
- Self-blame intensifies.
- Emotional pain increases.

Emotional Reframing Examples

Instead of: "I shouldn't feel this angry."
Try: "Anger is a natural response to loss and pain."

Instead of: "This sadness means I'm weak."
Try: "My grief reflects the depth of my love."

Instead of: "I must suppress these feelings."
Try: "I can acknowledge feelings without being controlled by them."

Disrupting harmful emotional patterns begins with recognizing what we're feeling and building the tools to respond thoughtfully. While we may not be able to prevent strong emotions from surfacing, we can change how we handle them—shifting from automatic reactions to more intentional, constructive responses.

> **EXERCISE: Emotion-Thought Mapping**
>
> - Identify a recent emotional trigger.
> - Notice the immediate emotion.
> - Track the thoughts that followed.
> - Observe your response/reaction.
> - Consider alternative perspectives.

Creating Emotional Space

Creating emotional space involves moving from automatic reaction to mindful response. First, we learn to recognize our emotions—naming them, sensing where they show up in our bodies, and acknowledging their presence. Next comes acceptance, where we allow feelings to exist without pushing them away or judging ourselves for having them. Finally, we choose how to respond, taking actions that reflect our values and long-term well-being while holding healthy boundaries.

Thomas shares his experience:

> *"I used to immediately act on my emotions—calling, texting, driving by my son's house. Learning to create space between feeling and action changed everything. Now I can feel the pain without making it worse through reactive behavior."*

> **EXERCISE: Creating Space Practice**
>
> When strong emotions arise:

- Pause and breathe.
- Name the emotion: "I am feeling . . ."
- Notice physical sensations.
- Rate intensity (1-10).
- Wait ninety seconds before acting.
- Choose a conscious response.

Building Resilient Thought Patterns

Developing more resilient thought patterns takes time and practice. It begins with intentionally shifting how we interpret challenges and setbacks. Instead of viewing difficult experiences—like estrangement—as personal failures or permanent conditions, resilient thinking invites us to acknowledge pain without becoming consumed by it. This means learning to recognize unhelpful mental habits, gently redirecting them, and creating space for both grief and forward movement.

Dr. Kristina Scharp explains:

> *"The goal isn't to eliminate the pain of estrangement, but rather to develop ways to cope with it that allow for both grieving and growth."*

Signs of Growing Resilience

- Quicker recovery from triggers.
- More balanced self-talk.
- Increased emotional regulation.
- Better boundary maintenance.
- Greater comfort with uncertainty.
- More flexible thinking.

Key Elements of Resilient Thinking:

1. Flexibility

    - Seeing multiple perspectives
    - Adjusting to new information

- Adapting responses as needed
- Maintaining emotional balance

2. Self-Compassion

   - Acknowledging human imperfection
   - Treating yourself with kindness
   - Recognizing shared experiences
   - Maintaining healthy boundaries

3. Reality-Based Hope

   - Accepting current circumstances
   - Identifying possible growth
   - Maintaining agency
   - Building meaningful life

Practical Applications

Sarah discovered the power of these techniques during a challenging holiday season:

> *"Instead of my usual spiral into shame and self-blame, I practiced reframing each difficult moment. When someone asked about my daughter, instead of thinking 'Everyone must judge me,' I reminded myself: 'Many parents face similar challenges, and others' opinions don't define my worth.'"*

Common Challenging Situations and Reframing Options

1. Family Gatherings

   Instead of: "I can't face everyone's questions."
   Try: "I can choose how much to share and set boundaries as needed."

2. Social Media

Instead of: "Everyone else has perfect relationships."
Try: "Social media shows partial stories, not complete realities."

3. Holidays

    Instead of: "This day is ruined forever."
    Try: "I can create new meanings and traditions."

4. Public Encounters

    Instead of: "I must explain everything."
    Try: "I can protect my privacy while being authentic."

Practicing these shifts in thinking *before* challenges arise builds essential mental resilience. Proactive preparation—rather than reactive coping—trains the brain to respond constructively under stress. When we rehearse alternative perspectives and responses during calm moments, we create neural pathways that become more accessible during stress. This is similar to how athletes visualize successful performances or emergency responders drill procedures—the repetition builds automatic, constructive responses that can override our typical fight-or-flight reactions.

By mentally practicing how to reframe a critical comment as feedback, or viewing a setback as a learning opportunity, we develop emotional resilience that kicks in precisely when we need it most. The key is specificity: rather than generic positive thinking, we prepare tailored responses to our known triggers, creating a mental toolkit that helps us respond thoughtfully instead of merely reacting emotionally.

EXERCISE: Situation-Specific Reframing

Choose three challenging situations you frequently face and then:

- Identify typical thought patterns.
- Create alternative perspectives.
- Practice new responses.
- Plan self-care strategies.
- Identify support resources.

> Remember: The goal isn't to avoid discomfort but to respond to it more effectively.

Daily Reframing Practice

To make reframing a natural response rather than a conscious effort, consider establishing daily practices. Real change happens through small daily habits, not big dramatic shifts. You might spend just two minutes each morning thinking about a challenge you'll face and how you could view it differently. Or end each day by finding one good thing about a tough moment you had. These quick, regular practices slowly change how your brain naturally thinks. Over time, looking at situations in a balanced way starts to feel automatic instead of forced.

The best part is that these small daily efforts add up. You're not constantly fighting against your old thinking patterns, which is exhausting. Instead, you're gradually training your mind to naturally handle difficult situations in a healthier way.

Regular practice helps balanced thinking become more natural over time. Real reframing means accepting difficult feelings like disappointment or hurt while also staying open to what you might learn or how things could improve. This keeps you from getting stuck in two unhelpful extremes: either feeling like a victim or pretending everything's fine when it's not.

In our example of Marcus above, being passed over for a promotion can feel scary and upsetting—and that's valid. At the same time, it might open doors to new career paths or help you develop new skills. You don't have to pick just one way of seeing it. You can hold both truths at once.

This balanced approach lets you fully feel your emotions while still believing you have some control over what happens next. You're not ignoring the hard stuff, but you're also not closing yourself off to possibilities.

As you practice reframing your thoughts, you may have noticed that some days feel easier than others. This variation is normal and

---

Daily Reframing Practice

Morning Practice:

❖ Set intention for balanced thinking.
❖ Review potential challenges.
❖ Prepare specific reframes.
❖ Connect with support resources.

Evening Review:

❖ Notice thought patterns.
❖ Celebrate successful reframes.
❖ Learn from difficulties.
❖ Plan for tomorrow.

expected. Any skill we want to develop takes time, consistency, and practice.

As Patricia reflects:

> "Some days reframing comes easily, others it feels impossible. I've learned to be gentle with myself while maintaining the practice. Over time, I've noticed my first thoughts becoming less harsh, my recovery from triggers quicker, and my overall perspective more balanced."

Creating Your Personal Thought Reframing Toolkit

Every parent's journey through estrangement is unique, and your reframing toolkit should reflect your specific needs and challenges. You won't need all the tools every day, but having more tools will give you more options for difficult days.

Essential Tools for Your Kit:

As a parent navigating the pain of estrangement, it's important to have practical tools you can turn to in moments of distress or uncertainty. Quick grounding techniques can help you stay centered during emotional spikes—simple practices like deep breathing, physical anchoring gestures (such as placing your hand over your heart), or holding a comfort object or meaningful photo can bring immediate relief. Short affirmations and brief meditation sessions also offer calm in overwhelming moments.

> **Building Your Emergency Kit**
>
> Keep readily available:
> - List of supportive friends to call.
> - Social gathering scripts.
> - Holiday coping strategies.
> - Trigger management plans.
> - Grounding objects.
> - Comfort activities.
> - Crisis hotline numbers.
> - Self-care supplies.
> - Positive memory tokens.
> - Journal.
> - List of comfort activities.

When facing specific challenges, such as social events or holidays, having situation-specific responses ready can make a significant difference. Prepare scripts for awkward or painful conversations, strategies for coping with holiday triggers, and personalized plans for managing emotional flashpoints. Don't forget to maintain a self-care routine and keep a list of supportive contacts—people you trust to help you stay grounded and remind you that you are not alone.

Emotional processing is an ongoing part of healing. Tools like journaling prompts can help you give voice to your feelings, while creative outlets such as drawing or painting offer expression beyond words. Movement practices—whether walking, stretching, or dancing—can shift emotional energy, and curated music playlists or time spent in nature can reconnect you to peace and perspective. Each tool in this kit is meant to support your emotional resilience and help you stay connected to yourself, even in the absence of your child.

Maria shares:

> *"I keep a small box with items that help me reframe difficult moments—a smooth stone to hold, a photo of myself doing something I love, and cards with my favorite reframing statements. Having these physical tools helps make the mental work more tangible."*

Common Challenges and Strategies

Even with practice, certain situations can challenge our reframing skills more than others. Having specific strategies for common challenges helps prevent emotional flooding and helps you maintain your peace.

1. Family Events

   Instead of: "Everyone will judge me."
   Try: "I can focus on meaningful connections with those present."
   Practical Steps:
   - Prepare brief, honest responses.
   - Plan exit strategies.
   - Identify supportive allies.

- Schedule recovery time.
- Practice self-compassion.

2. Social Media Encounters

    Instead of: "Their life is perfect without me."
    Try: "Social media shows carefully curated moments, not full reality."
    Practical Steps:
    - Set viewing boundaries.
    - Use blocking tools.
    - Create alternative activities.
    - Connect with support groups.
    - Practice digital self-care.

3. Holiday Seasons

    Instead of: "This season is ruined forever."
    Try: "I can create new meanings and traditions."
    Practical Steps:
    - Design new rituals.
    - Connect with chosen family.
    - Focus on giving to others.
    - Honor your feelings.
    - Plan meaningful activities.

> **Signs of Growing Mastery**
>
> You're developing stronger reframing skills when:
>
> ❖ Recovery from triggers happens faster
> ❖ First thoughts become less harsh
> ❖ Self-compassion comes more naturally
> ❖ Boundaries feel clearer
> ❖ Hope feels more accessible
> ❖ Flexibility increases

EXERCISE: Situation Planning

Choose an upcoming challenging situation:

- Identify potential triggers.
- List automatic thoughts.
- Create reframing options.
- Plan coping strategies.
- Arrange support systems.

By practicing these situations, you won't prevent all difficult feelings, but you will respond with greater awareness and self-compassion. Over time, you may notice patterns in both progress and challenges. Tracking these patterns in your journal will help build confidence and identify areas needing additional support.

Thomas reflects:

> *"Looking back at my journal from six months ago, I can see how my automatic thoughts have shifted. The pain isn't gone, but I'm better at holding it without drowning in it."*

Working with Setbacks

Setbacks are a normal part of developing any new skill, including reframing. How we handle setbacks often matters more than the setbacks themselves. Each new challenge offers a chance to extend ourselves grace and renew our commitment to healing.

Dr. Joshua Coleman notes:

> *"Recovery from estrangement isn't linear. Setbacks are not only*

> *normal but can be valuable opportunities for deeper understanding and strengthening your coping skills."*

When Setbacks Occur:

1. Acknowledge without judgment.

   - Notice what happened.
   - Allow feelings to exist.
   - Avoid self-criticism.
   - Remember your humanity.

2. Assess with curiosity.

   - What triggered the setback?
   - What supports were missing?
   - What can be learned?
   - What needs attention?

3. Adjust and continue.

   - Review helpful tools.
   - Strengthen supports.
   - Modify strategies.
   - Recommit to practice.

Remember: Setbacks don't erase progress—they're opportunities for deeper learning and growth. As you become more skilled at basic reframing, they become natural, automatic responses.

Creating Supportive Environments

The spaces around us can either make it easier or harder to think in healthy ways. When we set up our surroundings thoughtfully, balanced thinking becomes more automatic. Your physical space matters—having calming colors, meaningful items that make you feel good, plants or natural elements, and comfort objects can all help create a peaceful atmosphere that supports clear thinking.

The people in your life are equally important: surrounding yourself with supportive friends, understanding family members, helpful professionals, and others who encourage growth while maintaining healthy boundaries creates a social environment that reinforces positive thinking patterns.

Even your digital world plays a role—being selective about social media feeds, joining positive online groups, bookmarking helpful resources, and choosing inspiring content can turn your phone and computer into tools that support rather than undermine your mental well-being.

When all these elements work together, reframing difficult situations becomes much more natural because your entire environment is gently encouraging balanced, constructive thinking rather than pulling you toward negativity or stress.

EXERCISE: Environment Assessment

Review your current environment:

1. What supports reframing?

   - Physical elements
   - People and relationships
   - Activities and routines
   - Resources and tools

2. What challenges reframing?

   - Triggering items
   - Difficult relationships
   - Unhelpful habits
   - Missing supports

3. What is my action plan?

   - Add supportive elements
   - Remove challenges
   - Strengthen boundaries
   - Build new routines

Linda shares:

> *"I realized my home was full of triggers—photos, objects, even furniture that sparked negative thoughts. I didn't get rid of*

everything, but I made certain spaces where I could practice reframing without constant emotional reminders."

While initial reframing focuses on managing daily emotions and immediate challenges, deeper work is about making peace with what happened to you without letting it take over your whole identity. Many parents struggling with estrangement find that the pain becomes so consuming it threatens to eclipse their other roles, achievements, and qualities—they stop seeing themselves as successful professionals, loving partners, devoted friends, or caring community members, instead viewing themselves primarily through the lens of being "the parent whose child won't speak to them."

Advanced reframing helps you see yourself as a whole person again by putting the estrangement into the bigger picture of your entire life, not just this one painful part. This involves recognizing how the experience has contributed to personal growth, empathy, and resilience while simultaneously honoring other identities and accomplishments. Rather than allowing estrangement to become the defining chapter, parents learn to see it as one significant experience among many that has shaped but not consumed their identity. This integration creates space for continued personal development, meaningful relationships, and purposeful living, even while the pain of separation remains real and valid.

EXERCISE: Identity Integration

Write about:

- How has estrangement changed you?

- What strengths have you discovered?

- What wisdom have you gained?

- What new possibilities exist?

- Who are you becoming?

As we conclude our exploration of reframing, remember that this work isn't about forcing positive thinking or denying pain—it's about developing a more flexible, compassionate way of understanding your experience.

Margaret, whom we met at the beginning of this chapter, reflects:

> *"Learning to reframe my thoughts about estrangement hasn't eliminated the pain, but it's given me tools to live with it more peacefully. I can hold both the grief and the possibility of growth."*

Key Takeaways:

- Reframing is a skill that develops with practice.
- Progress isn't linear—setbacks are normal and expected.
- Multiple perspectives can coexist.
- Self-compassion supports effective reframing.
- Your toolkit should be personalized to your needs.
- Environmental support enhances reframing success.

Healthy reframing doesn't mean pushing away sadness, anger, or grief, or pretending that everything is okay when it clearly isn't. Instead, it's about learning to experience difficult feelings while also keeping room in your mind for kindness toward yourself and belief that things can improve. Think of it like being able to hold two things at once—you can fully feel the hurt of your situation while also treating yourself with the same compassion you'd show a good friend going through hard times.

This kind of mental flexibility helps you say, "Yes, this hurts," and at the same time, "I'm still a person who matters and who can get through this."

It's not about choosing between feeling bad or staying hopeful. It's about making room for both—honestly facing the pain while also showing yourself compassion as you heal. This balance helps you process what you're feeling and keep moving forward.

In our next chapter, we'll deepen our exploration of self-compassion, building on the reframing skills you've developed here. We'll learn specific techniques for treating ourselves with the same kindness we'd offer a friend facing similar challenges. You'll discover how self-compassion can transform your relationship with yourself while navigating the complex emotions of estrangement.

National Crisis Hotline

If you're experiencing thoughts of self-harm or feeling overwhelmed call:

988
or
1-800-273-8255

Available 24/7 for support and guidance.

Remember: You can always pause, take a break, or seek additional support when needed. Your emotional safety comes first.

CHAPTER 6:

Cultivating Kindness—The Practice of Self-Compassion

Sarah stands before her bathroom mirror, tears streaming down her face after another sleepless night. The familiar critical voice in her head starts its usual litany: "Why can't you just move on? What kind of mother are you?" But today, something shifts. She places a trembling hand over her heart, meets her own gaze in the mirror, and whispers, "This is so hard. You're doing the best you can." This simple act of self-kindness—treating herself with the same compassion she'd offer a friend—marks the beginning of a transformative journey.

For many parents experiencing estrangement, self-compassion feels not just difficult but almost wrong. We've been conditioned to believe that being hard on ourselves somehow makes us better parents or people. The pain of estrangement often amplifies this inner critic, turning everyday moments into opportunities for harsh self-judgment.

Dr. Kristin Neff, a leading researcher in self-compassion, explains:

> *"Self-compassion isn't about letting ourselves off the hook or avoiding responsibility. It's about treating ourselves with the same kindness we'd extend to a good friend going through difficulty."*

This distinction is crucial for parents navigating estrangement, where the line between healthy accountability and destructive self-blame often becomes blurred.

Think about how you respond when a close friend faces a crisis. You likely offer understanding, patience, and support. You remind them of their strengths while acknowledging their pain. Yet when facing our own struggles with estrangement, many of us default to harsh criticism and judgment. We tell ourselves we should be "over it by now" or that we must have failed completely as parents to end up in this situation.

Margaret discovered this disconnect during a support group meeting.

> *"I was comforting another mother who was blaming herself for her daughter's estrangement, telling her how complex family relationships are and how we all do our best with what we know at the time. Then I realized—I never extend that same understanding to myself. I'm either the worst mother ever or I'm trying to pretend everything's fine. There's no middle ground."*

This tendency to bounce between extreme self-judgment and forced positivity is common. True self-compassion offers a different path—one that acknowledges both our humanity and our pain. It creates space for genuine healing by allowing us to be honest about our struggles while maintaining our basic sense of worthiness as people and parents.

Research on estrangement shows that many parents initially resist self-compassion, believing they deserve their pain or that being kind to themselves means excusing past mistakes. However, creating emotional safety through self-compassion actually enables parents to examine difficult truths and make meaningful changes.

Dr. Joshua Coleman observes in *Rules of Estrangement*:

> *"Many parents resist self-compassion because they believe they deserve to suffer. Yet self-punishment rarely leads to the kind of growth and healing that might actually help repair the relationship."*

Understanding True Self-Compassion

Let's be clear about what self-compassion is and isn't. Self-compassion is not:

- Feeling sorry for yourself.
- Making excuses for past actions.
- Ignoring areas that need growth.
- Pretending everything is fine.
- Giving up on reconciliation.

Instead, self-compassion means:

- Acknowledging pain without drowning in it.
- Taking responsibility without shame.
- Learning from mistakes while maintaining self-respect.
- Holding hope while accepting current reality.
- Caring for yourself while navigating difficulty.

Thomas shares his journey:

> "I used to think being hard on myself would somehow fix things—like if I punished myself enough, my son would come back. Learning self-compassion helped me see that beating myself up just left me too exhausted to do the real work of healing and growth."

The Science of Self-Kindness

Research shows that people who practice self-compassion demonstrate greater emotional resilience, better relationship skills, and more effective problem-solving abilities.

Developing self-compassion helps parents:

- Better manage overwhelming emotions.
- Set healthy boundaries while maintaining hope for connection.
- Process grief without becoming trapped in shame.

- Make positive changes without harsh self-judgment.
- Handle social situations with greater confidence.

Most importantly, self-compassion provides a foundation for authentic healing. When we're constantly attacking ourselves, we stay trapped in cycles of shame that make genuine growth impossible. Self-compassion creates the emotional safety needed to honestly examine our situations, accept responsibility where appropriate, and make meaningful changes.

Patricia discovered this truth through her own experience:

> *"I spent two years trying to force myself to 'get over it' through sheer willpower. All that did was make me feel worse about still hurting. When I finally learned to be gentle with myself, I could actually feel my feelings without being consumed by them. That's when real healing began."*

Getting Started with Self-Compassion

The journey to self-compassion often begins with small moments of conscious kindness. Just as Sarah did in our opening scene, we can practice pausing when we notice self-critical thoughts and choosing a more compassionate response. This doesn't mean ignoring difficult feelings or pretending everything is fine. Instead, we're learning to hold our pain with understanding rather than judgment. Look for natural opportunities throughout your day to practice kindness toward yourself.

Thomas shares his small moments:

> *"I began with my morning coffee routine. Instead of immediately*

Quick Self-Compassion Moments

❖ Morning Mirror Practice: Meet your eyes with kindness.
❖ Commute Check-in: Three deep breaths at stoplights.
❖ Meal-time Pause: Brief gratitude moment.
❖ Evening Wind-down: Gentle self-acknowledgment.
❖ Trigger Response: Hand-on-heart technique.

> *checking my phone or dwelling on problems, I'd take those few minutes to place a hand on my heart and say something encouraging to myself. Just like I'd say to a friend: 'You're doing the best you can with a really tough situation.'"*

Dr. Kristin Neff recommends:

> *"Start with small moments of self-kindness throughout your day. These 'self-compassion breaks' help build the habit of treating yourself with care, especially during difficult times."*

Self-compassion breaks are brief moments throughout the day when we intentionally offer ourselves kindness. It's like filling your proverbial bucket, a drop at a time, building a reserve of emotional energy for when we need it.

Linda shares how she began:

> *"I started with just one moment each morning. Before looking at my phone or thinking about the day ahead, I'd put my hand on my heart and say, 'May I be kind to myself today.' It felt awkward at first, even silly. But gradually, it became a touchstone I could return to when things got hard."*

This practice might feel unnatural at first, especially if you're used to being your own harshest critic. That's normal. Remember, we're working to develop a new skill—one that may feel foreign after years of self-judgment. Just as you'd be patient with a friend learning something new, try to be patient with yourself in this process.

Building Your Self-Compassion Practice

As we begin developing self-compassion, it's helpful to understand the three core elements that Dr. Kristin Neff has identified through her research: mindfulness, common humanity, and self-kindness. These components work together to create a more balanced and nurturing relationship with ourselves.

Mindfulness comes first—we need to notice our pain before we can respond to it with kindness. Many parents experiencing estrangement try to push away their difficult feelings, believing they should "be stronger" or "get over it." But true healing starts with acknowledging where we are right now, without judgment.

Maria describes her experience:

> *"I used to wake up every morning trying to convince myself I was fine. It was exhausting, and it never worked. Learning to simply say 'Yes, this hurts right now' actually helped me feel less overwhelmed by the pain. It sounds strange, but accepting the difficulty made it more manageable."*

The second element, common humanity, reminds us that suffering is a shared human experience. When we're going through something as painful as estrangement, we often feel isolated—like we're the only ones who have failed so completely as parents. But millions of families experience estrangement. Recognizing this doesn't minimize our personal pain, but it helps us feel less alone and ashamed.

Dr. Karl Pillemer notes in *Fault Lines*:

> *"When estranged parents realize how common their experience is, it often helps reduce their sense of isolation and shame. Understanding that other caring, well-intentioned parents face similar challenges can be the first step toward healing."*

Self-kindness, the third element, means treating ourselves with the same care we'd offer a dear friend. This doesn't mean excusing mistakes or avoiding responsibility. Instead, it means addressing our challenges with understanding rather than harsh judgment.

Sarah shares how she developed this voice:

> *"I started by imagining how my grandmother would speak to me—she was always kind but honest. When I catch myself being harsh, I try to channel her gentle wisdom instead."*

Thomas shares how this shift changed his healing journey:

> *"I realized I was talking to myself in ways I'd never speak to*

> *anyone else. When I started treating myself like I'd treat a friend going through the same situation—with patience, understanding, and encouragement—I could finally start processing my grief instead of just beating myself up about it."*

Self-compassion grows stronger through regular practice. Start with small, manageable moments throughout the day. These brief pauses for self-kindness can gradually reshape how we relate to ourselves during difficult times.

The Power of Sensory Support

Dr. Kristin Neff's research shows that engaging our physical senses through self-soothing touch and gentle movement can help bypass mental self-criticism and activate our natural caregiving response. When we're stuck in a loop of being hard on ourselves, one of the quickest ways to feel kinder toward ourselves is by connecting to our senses—like touching something soft, smelling something relaxing, or listening to gentle music.

Touch can help calm us down by activating the part of the nervous system that tells the body it's safe. This is called the parasympathetic nervous system. One simple practice involves placing a hand on your heart or giving yourself a soft hug when you notice you're being self-critical. This physical gesture of self-soothing, combined with kind words like "This is really hard right now" or "I'm here with you in this pain," can help interrupt patterns of harsh self-judgment.

> **Self-Soothing Gestures**
>
> Gentle ways to offer yourself physical comfort:
>
> ❖ Hand on heart.
> ❖ Crossed arms self-hug.
> ❖ Gentle shoulder squeeze.
> ❖ Soft face or neck massage.
> ❖ Rhythmic breathing with touch.

These physical gestures might feel strange at first, but they serve as powerful anchors for self-compassion practice. They give us something tangible to do when emotions feel overwhelming, helping to break the cycle of mental self-attack. These small actions can also cause your body to release oxytocin, a natural chemical that makes you feel comforted and cared for.

Patricia found this approach particularly helpful during holidays:

> "I keep lavender oil in my purse now. When family gatherings get overwhelming, I step away for a moment, put a drop on my wrist, and breathe deeply. The familiar scent helps me remember my self-compassion practice when emotions are running high."

Another approach involves writing yourself short notes of encouragement, the way you might write to a friend in crisis. Keep these notes where you can easily find them during difficult times—on your nightstand, in your wallet, or saved on your phone. They serve as tangible reminders to treat yourself with compassion when pain feels overwhelming.

The key is consistency rather than perfection. You don't have to transform your entire relationship with yourself overnight. Small acts of self-kindness, practiced regularly, gradually create new patterns of self-relating that support healing rather than hinder it.

Breaking Through Common Barriers

Many parents initially resist self-compassion, fearing it means letting themselves "off the hook" or giving up hope for reconciliation. Understanding and addressing these concerns is crucial for developing a sustainable self-compassion practice.

Linda expresses a common worry:

> "At first, I thought being kind to myself meant I was accepting that the estrangement was okay or that I didn't care anymore. I had to learn that self-compassion actually helps me stay present with my pain without being destroyed by it."

Self-compassion doesn't mean avoiding responsibility or resisting growth. Instead, it offers emotional safety that allows us to see our actions more clearly.

Dr. Joshua Coleman writes in *Rules of Estrangement*:

> *"Self-compassion allows parents to look at their role in the estrangement without drowning in shame or self-recrimination. It creates a foundation of emotional safety from which real change becomes possible."*

This is particularly important for parents of estranged adult children, who often carry deep wells of rootless guilt and shame. Self-compassion doesn't ask us to ignore mistakes or pretend everything is fine. Instead, it allows us to acknowledge both our humanness and our capacity for growth.

By treating ourselves with kindness, we create an internal environment where honest self-reflection becomes possible. This gentler approach actually supports deeper healing and positive change, while constant self-criticism tends to keep us stuck in cycles of shame and reactivity.

When Sarah first started practicing self-compassion, she felt awkward and resistant. "It seemed selfish somehow," she recalls, "like I was letting myself off the hook for my part in the estrangement." But as she continued the practice, she discovered something surprising: being kinder to herself actually made it easier to examine difficult truths about her relationship with her daughter.

This is what some call a "compassion paradox"—when we create a safe internal environment through self-kindness, we become more capable of honest self-reflection and meaningful change. It's like having a wise, supportive friend living inside your mind, one who can both comfort you and gently guide you toward growth.

Building a Daily Practice

While spontaneous moments of self-kindness are valuable, developing a regular practice helps build the neural pathways that make self-compassion more automatic. Many therapists recommend starting with just five minutes each day, perhaps as part of your morning or evening routine.

This might involve:

- A brief self-compassion meditation
- Writing a kind note to yourself

- Practicing gentle self-touch
- Speaking encouraging words aloud
- Simply sitting quietly with whatever you're feeling

The goal isn't to fix or change your emotions, but to create a compassionate space for whatever you're experiencing.

As Sarah discovered:

> *"When I stopped trying to force myself to feel better and just sat with my feelings with kindness, healing started happening naturally."*

Remember, this practice isn't about achieving some perfect state of self-love. It's about developing a more supportive relationship with yourself, especially during difficult times. Just as you wouldn't expect a friend to transform overnight, be patient with yourself as you develop this new skill.

Neuroscience research shows that repeated practice of self-compassion creates new neural pathways in the brain. Each time we choose self-kindness over self-criticism, we strengthen our capacity for emotional resilience.

Dr. Kristin Neff explains:

> *"Self-compassion is like a muscle that gets stronger with use. The more we practice treating ourselves with kindness, the more natural and automatic it becomes. While it doesn't eliminate our pain, it changes our relationship to suffering."*

Creating Safe Spaces for Practice

It's important to have physical spaces where you feel secure enough to practice self-compassion. This might be a corner of your bedroom, a comfortable chair, or even your car during your morning commute. The key is finding places where you can pause, breathe, and turn your attention inward with kindness.

Margaret created what she calls her "comfort corner" in her home office:

> "I have a soft blanket, some family photos that make me smile, and a journal where I write kind messages to myself. When things get overwhelming, I know I have this space where I can go to practice being gentle with myself."

EXERCISE: Design A Comfort Space

1. Choose a location in your home.
2. List comforting items to include:

   - Soft textures (blanket, pillow)
   - Meaningful photos or objects
   - Soothing scents
   - Calming colors
   - Journal and pen

   _____

   _____

   _____

3. Set up your space.
4. Create a simple ritual for using it.

Beyond setting up one dedicated space for self-compassion, parents should think about making their whole home more emotionally supportive. When you're surrounded by things that constantly remind you of your struggles and heartaches, it becomes much harder to break free from negative thinking patterns and be kind to yourself.

Your physical environment directly affects your emotional well-being. The spaces where you spend time each day can either fuel self-criticism or help you feel more at peace. Small changes—like temporarily storing photos that bring up painful memories or removing constant visual reminders of your child's absence—can make a surprising difference in how you feel about yourself throughout the day. This doesn't mean erasing your child from your life, but rather creating breathing room where you can practice self-compassion without being overwhelmed by grief and regret.

Maria discovered this truth when reorganizing her home:

> *"I realized certain spaces were full of triggers that sparked self-criticism. I didn't remove all the family photos, but I created some rooms that felt like peaceful sanctuaries where I could practice being kind to myself."*

EXERCISE: Environmental Assessment

Take stock of your surroundings:

- Notice what supports self-compassion.

_____

_____

_____

- Identify what triggers harsh self-judgment.

_____

_____

_____

- Make small adjustments to create more supportive spaces.
- Include elements that remind you to be kind to yourself.

Working with Difficult Emotions

One of the most challenging aspects of self-compassion practice is learning to stay present with painful feelings without getting lost in them. Think of emotions like weather patterns—they move through us, sometimes intensely, but they don't last forever. Studies on emotional regulation show that self-compassion helps us weather emotional storms by allowing us to stay present with our feelings rather than fighting or fleeing from them.

Patricia found this metaphor particularly helpful:

> *"Instead of berating myself for still feeling sad three years into estrangement, I learned to say, 'Of course this hurts. I'm weathering an emotional storm right now, and that's okay. This too shall pass.'"*

EXERCISE: Weather Pattern Practice

When strong emotions arise:

- Name the "weather" (emotional state).
- Notice where you feel it in your body.
- Remind yourself: "This will pass."
- Use gentle touch or words for comfort.
- Track how the feeling changes.

Using Your Self-Compassion Tools: Working Through Challenges

Many parents find that their self-compassion practice flows smoothly during calm moments but becomes challenging when triggers arise.

Sarah discovered this when she unexpectedly saw her daughter's picture on a mutual friend's social media post.

> *"All my practice seemed to vanish in that moment. The harsh self-talk came flooding back."*

This experience is entirely normal. Think of self-compassion as a muscle—it grows stronger with consistent use, but it can feel unsteady when first put to the test during stressful moments. The important thing is to begin with small challenges and gradually work your way up to more difficult ones.

Working with Triggers

Common triggers for parents experiencing estrangement often include:

- Special occasions and holidays
- Family gatherings
- Social media encounters
- Seeing other families together
- Well-meaning questions from friends
- Memories or photographs
- Birthday and anniversary dates

Rather than trying to avoid these triggers (which isn't usually possible), we can prepare for them with specific self-compassion tools.

Thomas shares how this works in practice:

> *"When I see fathers with their sons at the hardware store, I used to spiral into shame and self-recrimination. Now I catch myself, put my hand on my heart, and say, 'Of course this hurts. Anyone would feel sad in this situation.' It doesn't take away the pain, but it helps me move through it with more grace."*

Quick Response Tool

When triggers arise:
1. Pause and breathe.
2. Place hand on heart.
3. Acknowledge the pain.
4. Offer gentle words.
5. Remember you're not alone.
6. Take care of immediate needs.

Working with Shame

Shame often presents the biggest barrier to self-compassion, especially for parents experiencing estrangement. Shame whispers that we're unworthy of kindness, that our suffering is the consequence of being "bad" parents. Overcoming it takes steady, compassionate persistence.

Dr. Joshua Coleman notes:

> *"Self-compassion allows us to look at our role in the estrangement without drowning in shame or self-recrimination."*

EXERCISE: Shame Dialogue Practice

When shame arises:

- Notice the shame message.
- Write it down.
- Respond as if to a friend.
- Create a compassionate alternative.
- Read both aloud.
- Notice which feels true.

For example:

Shame says: "You must be a terrible mother if your child won't speak to you."
Compassionate response: "Parenting is complex, and many good parents face estrangement. Your pain shows how much you care."

Linda found this practice transformative:

> *"Writing down my shame thoughts and then responding with compassion helped me see how harsh I was being with myself. Would I ever say these things to another parent in my situation? Never."*

Building Your Emergency Kit

Just as you might keep a first-aid kit for physical injuries, having a self-compassion emergency kit can help during emotional difficulties.

EXERCISE: Creating Your Comfort Kit

Gather items that support self-compassion:

- A small smooth stone or comfort object
- A written list of kind self-statements
- Photos that make you smile
- A favorite scent
- Emergency contact numbers
- Brief meditation scripts
- Comfort music playlist

Keep your comfort kit somewhere you can reach it easily—whether that's in your bag, your car, or a desk drawer. Unlike a designated compassion corner that requires you to relocate, this kit is portable and immediate. Its presence offers a tangible reminder to pause, breathe, and treat yourself with kindness, right in the moment when you need it most.

Handling Setbacks

Every parent experiences moments when self-compassion feels impossible. As we've discussed previously, setbacks aren't failures—they're some of the most vital opportunities to practice self-compassion. The way we respond to ourselves in moments of struggle is just as important as the act of self-compassion itself.

Patricia remembers:

> *"During my daughter's wedding, which I wasn't invited to, all*

> *my practice seemed useless. I fell into old patterns of self-blame and shame."*

When self-compassion feels difficult, start by acknowledging that it *is* hard—and that's okay. Remind yourself that struggling in this way is a normal part of being human. Then begin again with the basic steps above. Offer yourself physical comfort, whether through a calming breath, a warm blanket, or placing a hand over your heart. Use simple, gentle phrases like "This is tough, but I'm doing my best." Don't hesitate to reach out for support.

Consistency matters more than perfection. Even small, repeated acts of self-kindness can reshape the brain, gradually forging new neural pathways that make compassion feel more natural and instinctive over time.

Remember Your Support Network

Self-compassion grows stronger when supported by understanding people. As I stressed in Chapters 1 and 2, creating a network of friends, family members, or support group participants who understand your journey can help maintain your practice during difficult times. If you haven't already identified people who you can turn to for help, please revisit those sections as you consider the people around you.

Remember: self-compassion isn't selfish—it's essential for healing. As you develop this practice, you're not just helping yourself; you're modeling a healthy self-relationship for others who might be struggling with similar challenges.

Building Your Support Circle

Remember to include people who:

- Understand estrangement
- Practice self-compassion
- Respect your journey
- Offer gentle encouragement
- Support your growth
- Honor your feelings

Moving Beyond Words

While affirmations and kind self-talk are valuable tools, many parents find that movement and creativity offer unique pathways to self-compassion. Sarah discovered this through simple walking meditation:

> *"Sometimes I just can't find the right words to comfort myself. On those days, I walk in nature, matching my breath to my steps. There's something about moving my body that helps me feel more compassionate toward myself."*

EXERCISE: Embodied Self-Compassion

Choose a simple physical activity like:

- Walking
- Gentle stretching
- Dancing to music
- Working in a garden
- Creating art

As you move, notice:

- The sensation of being in your body
- Your breath flowing naturally
- Any tension releasing
- Moments of peace or pleasure
- Connection to the present moment

Working with Deep Pain

Some moments in estrangement cut particularly deep—missed weddings, births of grandchildren, holiday absences. These times require especially tender self-compassion practice. Rather than minimizing such profound losses, we can learn to hold them with the gentleness they deserve, acknowledging our pain while caring for ourselves through it.

Thomas describes his approach:

> "When my son got married without telling me, I wanted to collapse into shame and self-recrimination. Instead, I tried something different. I lit a candle, acknowledged my deep sadness, and spoke to myself as I would to another father in my situation: 'This hurts terribly, and that's natural. You can hold both your love for your son and your pain at missing this moment.'"

EXERCISE: Holding Difficult Moments

When facing particularly painful situations:
- Create a quiet, safe space.
- Acknowledge the specific pain.
- Offer yourself physical comfort (hand on heart, gentle touch).
- Speak to yourself with deep understanding.
- Allow whatever emotions arise.
- Remember you're not alone in this experience.

Integrating Self-Compassion into Daily Life

As your practice deepens, you'll likely find opportunities to bring self-compassion into everyday moments. Research indicates that with practice, self-compassion can become a natural response rather than a conscious effort.

Linda describes this evolution:

> "Now when I see a mother and daughter shopping together, instead of immediately attacking myself, my first response is

> *usually a gentle acknowledgment: 'Yes, this triggers sadness, and that's okay.' It's becoming more automatic, like muscle memory."*

Looking to the Future

One of the most challenging aspects of estrangement is maintaining hope while accepting current reality. Self-compassion helps create space for both. True self-compassion gives us room to accept the full range of human experience. It lets us long for healing or restoration while also caring for what we have now. These aren't opposing forces. Instead, self-compassion helps us see that we can hope for the future and still invest in our present relationships, goals, and growth.

> **Signs of Integration**
>
> You may notice:
> - ❖ Quicker recovery from triggers.
> - ❖ More natural self-soothing responses.
> - ❖ Decreased harsh self-talk.
> - ❖ Greater emotional resilience.
> - ❖ More balanced perspective on challenges.
> - ❖ Increased capacity for joy despite pain.

Margaret shares her experience:

> *"Learning to be kind to myself helped me see that I don't have to choose between hoping for a relationship with my daughter and taking care of myself now. Both can exist together, held in compassion."*

EXERCISE: Future-Focused Compassion

Consider:

- What would your compassionate self say about your hopes?

_____

_____

- How can you honor both your wishes and your current needs?

  _____

  _____

  _____

- What small steps might support your healing journey?

  _____

  _____

  _____

- What possibilities remain open even within current limitations?

  _____

  _____

  _____

  _____

Remember: The future remains unwritten, and your commitment to self-compassion creates space for healing—whatever form that may take. Dr. Joshua Coleman notes:

> *"Clinical experience shows that parents who develop self-compassion are better equipped to handle the emotional challenges of estrangement while maintaining hope for healing."*

As your self-compassion practice deepens, you may notice subtle shifts in how you relate to yourself and your estrangement experience. Linda describes this evolution:

> "It wasn't like flipping a switch—more like watching a sunrise. Gradually, I realized I could hold my sadness with gentleness instead of pushing it away or drowning in it."

Embracing Self-Compassion as a Way of Life

The key to long-term success with self-compassion lies in developing practices that feel natural and sustainable. In other words, don't force yourself to meditate for long periods or complete elaborate rituals. Instead, weave self-kindness into your regular routine—a gentle word while making coffee, a moment of acknowledgment before bed.

As we conclude our exploration of self-compassion, let's return to Sarah, whom we met at the beginning of this chapter.

Six months after that tearful morning in front of her mirror, Sarah reflects:

Signs of Growing Self-Compassion

You might notice:
- Automatic kind responses to difficulty.
- Quicker recovery from emotional triggers.
- More balanced self-talk.
- Increased emotional resilience.
- Better boundary maintenance.
- Greater comfort with uncertainty.

> "Self-compassion hasn't eliminated my pain, but it's given me a different way to carry it. I'm learning to be both strong and gentle with myself—something I never knew was possible."

This transformation illustrates the profound impact that self-compassion can have on our journey through estrangement. Remember that self-compassion is a skill that grows stronger with use. Some days it will flow naturally; others will challenge everything you've learned. Both experiences are normal and valuable parts of the journey.

Key Takeaways:

- Start where you are—every moment offers a new opportunity to choose kindness toward yourself.
- Honor your pace—healing unfolds differently for everyone—trust your own timing.
- Welcome imperfection—self-compassion includes accepting that we won't always get it right.
- Maintain connection—seek support from others who understand and respect your journey.
- Keep perspective—today's struggles don't define your entire story.

In our next chapter, we'll explore how self-compassion supports setting healthy limits while maintaining openness to possibility. You'll learn specific techniques for navigating relationships, managing expectations, and building a meaningful life that honors both your pain and your potential.

National Crisis Hotline

If you're experiencing thoughts of self-harm or feeling overwhelmed call:

988

or

1-800-273-8255

Available 24/7 for support and guidance.

Remember: You're not alone. Reaching out for help is an act of self-compassion.

CHAPTER 7:

Setting Boundaries— Navigating the Present Reality

Linda stands in the grocery store, frozen in the produce section. Her estranged daughter's best friend has just spotted her and is heading her way, wearing that look of determined curiosity Linda has come to recognize. In the past, such encounters would send her into a panic—either fleeing the store or getting trapped in a painful conversation that left her emotionally drained for days.

But today feels different. Drawing on her growing self-compassion practice, Linda takes a deep breath and recalls her prepared boundary statement. When Sarah reaches her and offers a friendly greeting, Linda smiles genuinely and says, "It's nice to see you."

As Sarah begins talking about Linda's daughter, Linda gently interrupts. "I'm really glad you two are still close," she says, "but I'm learning to keep family matters private these days."

The interaction is over in seconds, and Linda continues selecting her apples, noting with quiet pride how her hands have barely started trembling.

This small moment represents a crucial milestone in navigating life during estrangement—the ability to maintain healthy boundaries while staying present and gracious. It's the kind of practical skill that can transform daily life from a minefield of potential triggers into a manageable landscape.

During estrangement, maintaining appropriate boundaries means finding balance between sharing and privacy, between staying connected and protecting emotional well-being.

Dr. Joshua Coleman explains:

> *"Parents often struggle to find the right balance between maintaining appropriate boundaries and completely withdrawing from life and relationships."*

Understanding Healthy Boundaries

Boundaries in estrangement serve multiple purposes. They protect your emotional energy, maintain privacy, respect your adult child's choices (even when those choices are painful), and create essential space for your own healing. Most importantly, healthy boundaries help you navigate daily life without constant emotional upheaval or re-injury.

It's helpful to distinguish between healthy boundaries and defensive walls. Healthy boundaries allow you to share selectively—choosing when, how, and with whom to be vulnerable. They help preserve emotional connections where possible, while still protecting your energy and supporting your healing. Importantly, they remain flexible and can shift as your needs or circumstances change.

In contrast, defensive walls block all sharing, create isolation, and often drain more energy than they save. They can prevent healing by keeping you emotionally stuck and tend to remain rigid, even when change might be helpful. Learning to set healthy boundaries instead of building walls is an act of care—for yourself and for the relationship, no matter where it currently stands.

Boundaries vs. Walls

Healthy Boundaries:

- ❖ Allow selective sharing
- ❖ Maintain connections
- ❖ Protect energy
- ❖ Support healing
- ❖ Remain flexible

Defensive Walls:

- ❖ Block all sharing
- ❖ Isolate completely
- ❖ Drain energy
- ❖ Prevent healing
- ❖ Stay rigid

Many parents fear that setting boundaries means closing the door on reconciliation. It can feel like drawing a line in the sand or giving up hope. But in reality, boundaries are not about shutting someone out—they're about protecting your own well-being while leaving room for healthy connection if and when it becomes possible.

Thomas shares his early struggles:

> *"I thought setting boundaries meant I was giving up on reconciliation. My therapist helped me understand that having clear boundaries actually creates safer space for potential future connection. It's like building a garden fence—it defines the space while allowing things to grow."*

Creating Your Boundary Framework

Every parent's situation is unique, requiring personalized boundaries that reflect their specific circumstances and needs. When you're navigating estrangement from an adult child, boundaries can be especially challenging—but also vital. They help you protect your mental health, preserve your dignity, and regain a sense of agency in a relationship that may feel out of your control.

For instance, some parents choose to stop checking their child's social media, realizing it only leads to emotional pain or false hope. Others find it necessary to let friends or relatives know they're not open to conversations speculating about the estrangement. One mother decided to stop rereading old text messages from her son late at night, recognizing it triggered a spiral of guilt and sleeplessness. Another father gently asked his sister to stop acting as a go-between, even though she meant well—he realized it was keeping him from fully accepting the space his child had requested.

Boundaries in estrangement aren't about giving up; they're about creating emotional safety while still leaving room for healing—yours and potentially the relationship's. Whether you're managing your own expectations or navigating how much to share with others, setting clear, compassionate boundaries is a powerful step toward regaining stability.

Dr. Kylie Agllias notes:

> *"Boundaries serve multiple functions during estrangement: they help manage social situations, protect emotional well-being, and maintain personal dignity."*

EXERCISE: Boundary Assessment

Take a moment to consider:

1. Where do you need stronger boundaries?

   - Social situations
   - Family events
   - Online spaces
   - Personal habits
   - Self-talk patterns

   _____

   _____

2. What makes maintaining boundaries difficult?

   - Fear of judgment
   - Hope for information
   - Guilt or shame
   - Others' pressure
   - Internal doubt

   _____

   _____

   _____

Margaret discovered the importance of this assessment after several painful holiday seasons:

> *"I realized I had clear boundaries for strangers but none for family members who wanted to 'help' by sharing information about my daughter. Learning to set loving limits with well-meaning relatives actually helped me feel more in control of my healing process."*

Building Your Boundary Tool Kit

Just as we developed self-compassion practices in the previous chapter, creating effective boundaries requires specific tools and techniques. Perhaps the most important tool for boundaries is prepared responses. These help parents maintain composure during unexpected encounters, reducing the likelihood of emotional overwhelm. If you haven't yet done the exercise on prepared statements in Chapter 2, now is a good time to revisit that section.

Dr. Karl Pillemer emphasizes:

> *"Having prepared responses for difficult encounters helps parents navigate challenging social situat`ions while maintaining their emotional equilibrium."*

Patricia found these templates invaluable:

> *"My prepared responses feel like carrying a shield—not to fight with, but to protect myself while staying engaged in life. I don't have to think up responses when I'm already emotional; I can just reach for words I've already chosen carefully."*

Quick Response Templates

For casual inquiries:
"Thanks for asking, but I'm more of a private person when it comes to family stuff."

For persistent questions:
"I appreciate your concern, but this isn't something I discuss."

For social media:
"I'm taking a break from online family updates."

For family events:
"I'll attend, but I'm not comfortable discussing [name's] absence."

This combination of clear boundaries and prepared responses creates a foundation for navigating daily life during estrangement. In the following sections, we'll explore more specific strategies for different situations and relationships, always balancing protection with connection, hope with reality.

The key is remembering that boundaries aren't about shutting down or shutting out—they're about creating safe space for both healing and potential future growth. As we continue through this chapter, we'll build on these basic concepts to develop more nuanced approaches for specific challenges while maintaining the self-compassion we've been cultivating.

Navigating Social Situations: Finding Your Balance

Social encounters often present some of the biggest challenges for parents experiencing estrangement. Whether it's a casual meeting at the grocery store, as Linda experienced, or more structured events like family gatherings, having clear strategies helps maintain emotional equilibrium while staying connected to community.

When parents become estranged from their children, their first reaction is often to pull away from friends, family, and social activities. It might seem safer to avoid questions or judgment, and staying isolated can feel like a way to protect themselves from more hurt. But over time, being alone usually makes the pain worse. Without support or connection, it's harder to process emotions and begin to heal from the loss.

Signs of Social Withdrawal

Watch for:

- ❖ Declining most invitations.
- ❖ Avoiding familiar places.
- ❖ Limiting conversations.
- ❖ Restricting activities.
- ❖ Making excuses to stay home.
- ❖ Feeling anxious about casual encounters.

Dr. Kristina Scharp observes:

> *"While initial withdrawal may feel protective, prolonged isolation often compounds the emotional impact of estrangement."*

Finding the right balance between protection and connection

requires practice and patience. It starts with small, intentional choices—like showing up to a familiar gathering, preparing a brief response for difficult questions, or even just making eye contact and smiling at a neighbor. These acts may feel minor, but they can gently reopen doors to connection without overwhelming emotional vulnerability.

Julie shares her experience:

> *"For months after my son stopped speaking to me, I avoided everyone except my closest friend. Eventually, I realized I was making my world smaller and smaller. Learning to navigate social situations with clear boundaries helped me reclaim parts of my life I thought I'd lost forever."*

Building Social Confidence

Beginning with manageable social situations helps build confidence and develop effective boundary-maintaining skills. Try to spend time with people or in situations where you feel mostly safe and in control. These low-stress encounters give you a chance to practice setting boundaries without feeling overwhelmed. Each time you succeed, it helps build your confidence and prepares you to handle harder or more emotional situations in the future.

Thomas found this approach helpful:

> *"I started with brief conversations at the gym—people I knew casually but not well enough to ask personal questions. It gave me a chance to practice my boundary statements without feeling overwhelmed. Each successful interaction made me feel more capable of handling bigger challenges."*

EXERCISE: Social Situation Mapping

List social situations from least to most challenging:

- Casual encounters (grocery store, gym, church)
- Brief friendly chats

- Small gatherings
- Family events
- Holiday celebrations

Choose one situation from your "least challenging" category to practice with this week.

Managing Digital Boundaries in a Connected World

In today's digital age, setting and maintaining boundaries isn't just about face-to-face interactions—it also includes how we navigate texts, emails, and social media. For parents estranged from their adult children, these forms of communication can be especially painful. Messages may be misunderstood, taken out of context, or shared in ways that feel hurtful or violating. Without the nuance of tone or body language, even simple exchanges can lead to more confusion or conflict. Digital spaces also expose you to constant reminders—photos, posts, or updates—that can reopen wounds or stir up grief when you least expect it. And because these platforms often feel less personal, it's easier—intentionally or not—for others to be sharp, dismissive, or even cruel. Protecting your emotional well-being means deciding when and how to engage online, and recognizing that sometimes, not responding at all is the healthiest boundary you can set.

Sarah shares her early struggles:

> *"Every time I opened Facebook, I'd find myself scrolling through old photos or checking my daughter's profile. It became an obsession that kept reopening wounds instead of letting them heal."*

When you're feeling hurt or triggered, it's easy to react impulsively—replying to a message right away, rereading old posts, or checking a child's social media for clues. But these actions often increase pain and regret. Having clear, predetermined boundaries can give you a sense of control in moments when emotions run high. Whether it's choosing not to respond immediately, limiting how often you check certain accounts, or deciding who you allow into your digital space, these guidelines help you navigate online interactions with more clarity and confidence. Instead of being swept up in emotional reactions, you're following a plan that protects your well-being.

EXERCISE: Digital Boundary Assessment

Review your digital presence:

1. Social Media Platforms

    - What brings comfort vs. pain?
    - Which need immediate attention?
    - What can wait?

2. Digital Communications

    - Which channels feel safe?
    - What needs limits?
    - Where are your triggers?

3. Online Memories

    - What to preserve?
    - What to archive?
    - What to remove?

Practical Digital Boundary Strategies

Social media can stir up powerful emotions, especially when updates—or the lack of them—remind you of what's missing. Some hurting parents feel compelled to unfriend or block their adult child right away, especially in the midst of fresh pain. While this response is completely understandable, it's often best approached as a long-term decision rather than an immediate reaction. In some cases—especially where there is ongoing abuse or manipulation—blocking may be the healthiest and safest choice. But when possible, consider gentler options like unfollowing without unfriending, which allows you to step back without permanently closing the door.

Muting posts or stories is another way to reduce emotional triggers without making visible changes to the connection. Many platforms also offer *filters* to manage what appears in your feed, and viewing time limits can help you create emotional breathing room. If you have memories or milestones you want to preserve privately, creating private albums can offer a place for reflection without public exposure.

Thomas developed what he calls his "digital sanctuary":

> *"I created one private album with select photos I can look at when I feel strong enough. Everything else is archived—not deleted, but not visible in my daily life. This gives me control over when and how I engage with memories."*

> **Digital Management Tools**
>
> **Social Media:**
> ❖ Unfollow without unfriending
> ❖ Use platform filters
> ❖ Set viewing time limits
> ❖ Create private albums
> ❖ Utilize muting features
>
> **Email/Messaging:**
> ❖ Create separate folders
> ❖ Set auto-filters
> ❖ Use delayed responses
> ❖ Maintain professional tone
> ❖ Keep records secure
>
> **Online Support:**
> ❖ Choose moderated groups
> ❖ Set sharing limits
> ❖ Maintain privacy
> ❖ Practice self-care
> ❖ Honor others' boundaries

When it comes to email or messaging, setting up separate folders and auto-filters can help reduce anxiety by organizing communication and creating mental distance. If you're unsure how to respond to a message, delaying your response can allow time for reflection. Maintaining a calm, professional tone helps prevent escalations and ensures your words are ones you can stand by later. If you are on a shared device, it's also wise to keep records secure from other users, not out of suspicion, but to safeguard clarity and protect your emotional space.

Online support groups can be lifelines—but not all are created equal. Choose moderated communities where respectful dialogue is encouraged and harmful behavior is addressed. Set sharing limits for yourself so you feel safe in your vulnerability, and always maintain your privacy by being selective with personal details. As you seek support, remember to practice self-care and honor others' boundaries just as you wish your own to be respected. These steps cultivate healthier spaces, both for you and those walking a similar path.

Managing Mutual Connections

Digital boundaries become particularly important when dealing with shared connections. When mutual friends or family members remain in contact with both you and your estranged child, the digital landscape can become emotionally fraught. Well-meaning posts, tags, or shared updates can unexpectedly reopen wounds or create confusion about where boundaries lie. In these moments, clear communication and proactive digital boundaries can help protect your emotional well-being while preserving other valuable relationships.

Patricia found herself struggling with this:

> *"Friends would tag photos or share updates about my son, not realizing how painful it was. I had to learn to communicate my needs clearly but kindly."*

Dr. Wilson suggests:

> *"Create a simple, clear statement about your digital preferences that you can share with close friends and family. This helps prevent unintended hurt while maintaining important relationships."*

Sample Digital Boundary Statement:

"I'm working on healing and need to carefully manage my online exposure to family matters. I appreciate your understanding in not sharing or tagging posts about [name]. Thank you for supporting my journey."

Managing Family Events

Family gatherings often present unique challenges, as relatives may feel entitled to information or updates about your estranged child. When you're navigating the pain of estrangement from an adult child, even well-intentioned questions or advice from family members can feel overwhelming. These moments—often meant to show concern or offer help—can unintentionally stir up guilt, shame, or emotional exhaustion. That's why it's so important to have thoughtful, practiced responses from your boundary toolkit at the ready. Clear, compassionate boundaries allow you to protect your emotional well-being without cutting off connection.

With a little preparation, you can respond in ways that honor both your own needs and your relationships with those who care about you—even when they don't fully understand what you're going through. As briefly mentioned in Chapter 2, a three-tier response system provides escalating levels of response that allow parents to navigate these interactions with grace and consistency.

The first tier involves offering a brief, general response that acknowledges the situation without providing details. A simple statement like "We're still working through things" serves as a gentle deflection that satisfies most people's curiosity without opening the door to further discussion. This response is honest yet vague enough to discourage follow-up questions while maintaining a civil tone.

> **Family Event Strategies**
>
> **Before the event:**
> - Plan arrival and departure times.
> - Prepare responses.
> - Identify support people.
> - Schedule recovery time.
> - Have an exit strategy.
>
> **During the event:**
> - Take breaks as needed.
> - Stay grounded in the present.
> - Maintain kind but firm boundaries.
> - Focus on positive connections.
> - Honor your limits.
>
> **After the event:**
> - Process emotions.
> - Celebrate successes.
> - Note what worked.
> - Adjust strategies.
> - Practice self-care.

When someone persists despite the initial response, the second tier involves being more direct about boundaries. A clear statement such as "I appreciate your concern, but I'm not discussing this right now" communicates that the topic is off-limits while still acknowledging the person's interest. This approach is firm but respectful, making it clear that continued questioning would be inappropriate.

The third tier comes into play when someone ignores the boundary-setting of the second response. At this point, physically removing oneself from the conversation becomes necessary. A polite excuse like "I need to step away for a moment" allows for a graceful exit without creating drama or conflict. This final step protects emotional well-being while maintaining relationships with other family members.

Having these three levels planned in advance removes the pressure of formulating responses in emotionally charged moments. Parents can enter family gatherings with confidence, knowing they have a clear strategy for handling difficult conversations. This preparation helps maintain composure and ensures consistent responses across different situations and family members.

The key to navigating social life during estrangement lies in finding balance between honoring your emotional needs and maintaining meaningful connections. As we continue exploring this theme, we'll look at more specific strategies for different types of social situations while building on the boundary and self-compassion work we've already discussed.

Managing Birthday Boundaries

Birthdays can stir up complex emotions for parents estranged from their adult children. These once-celebratory milestones may now feel bittersweet, painful, or even hollow. Navigating these days requires intention, compassion, and often, new traditions. Whether it's your child's birthday or your own, managing expectations and setting healthy boundaries can be a crucial part of healing. Finding a personal way to honor the day—without reopening old wounds—can offer both comfort and clarity.

Linda describes her evolution in handling her daughter's birthday:

> "The first year, I tried to ignore it completely—that didn't work. Now I have a private ritual: I light a candle, write her a letter I may never send, and then do something nurturing for myself. It acknowledges both my love and my need for self-care."

Boundaries in Handling Major Life Events

Major life events in an estranged adult child's world—weddings, graduations, the birth of a grandchild—can bring a fresh wave of grief, especially when discovered indirectly. These milestones, once anticipated with joy, may now trigger feelings of exclusion, loss, and powerlessness. Setting boundaries around how you engage with such events, and how you care for yourself afterward, is essential. Having a plan for emotional support and self-care can make all the difference in navigating these painful moments with resilience and grace.

Margaret shares her experience:

> "Finding out about my grandson's birth through Facebook was devastating. My therapist helped me develop a response plan for such discoveries, including who to call and how to care for myself in the immediate aftermath."

Use the following framework to build your personal response plan:

Birthday Strategy Options

For Your Adult Child's Birthday:

- ❖ Acknowledge day privately.
- ❖ Plan for self-care.
- ❖ Seek emotional support.
- ❖ Reinforce boundaries.
- ❖ Plan alternative activities.

For Your Own Birthday:

- ❖ Make new traditions.
- ❖ Invite "chosen" family.
- ❖ Create personal rituals.
- ❖ Reflect on growth.
- ❖ Plan future celebrations.

EXERCISE: Creating Your Event Response Plan

1. **Immediate Response:**
   These are the tools and actions you can turn to in the moment of discovery to help stabilize your emotions and stay grounded.

   - Who can I contact right away for emotional safety? (e.g., a trusted friend, therapist)

     _____

   - What grounding techniques help me stay present? (e.g., deep breathing, holding an object, movement)

     _____

     _____

   - Where can I go to be alone if I need space?

     _____

   - What comfort activities soothe me? (e.g., tea, journaling, a walk, music)

     _____

     _____

   - What resources can I access? (e.g., support group, helpline, coping tools)

     _____

     _____

2. Short-Term Coping:
   Once the initial wave has passed, turn toward short-term strategies to help you process and stabilize.

   - How will I process my emotions? (e.g., writing, therapy, spiritual practice)

     _____

     _____

   - What does my body need? (e.g., sleep, food, movement)

     _____

     _____

   - Who can support me socially—without judgment or advice?

     _____

     _____

   - Do I need professional support to work through this?

     _____

   - How can I reinforce my boundaries? (e.g., limiting social media, deciding who to tell)

     _____

     _____

3. **Long-Term Integration:**
   Over time, you can reshape your relationship with the event in a way that supports your healing and growth.

   - How do I want to remember or relate to this event?

     _____

     _____

   - Can I find meaning in what happened, even if it's painful?

     _____

     _____

   - Has this changed how I see myself or my role?

     _____

     _____

   - What do I want to carry forward into the future?

     _____

     _____

   - What helps me hold on to hope?

     _____

     _____

Boundaries with Your Estranged Adult Child

Setting boundaries with an estranged adult child can feel counterintuitive—after all, aren't boundaries something that might push them further away? In reality, healthy boundaries in regards to our child are also essential for your well-being and may actually create the foundation for a healthier relationship in the future. When you allow yourself to be used, manipulated, or abused, you're not helping anyone heal or grow.

Understanding the Patterns

Many estranged adult children maintain contact primarily when they need something—financial help, childcare, or other support. They may reach out during crises, emergencies, or when other support systems have failed them. While your parental instincts naturally want to help, consistently being treated as a resource rather than a person damages both your well-being and any potential for genuine reconciliation.

Sarah remembers:

> "My daughter hadn't spoken to me in eight months when she called at midnight needing $800 for car repairs. When I asked if we could talk about our relationship first, she said, 'This isn't about that—do you want to help me or not?' I realized I had trained her to see me as an ATM, not a person. That night, I decided things had to change."

Some adult children use their own children as leverage, knowing that grandparents' love creates vulnerability. They may offer or withdraw access to grandchildren based on whether parents comply with their demands. This manipulation is particularly painful because it weaponizes the very relationships that bring you joy and meaning.

Julie remembers:

> "My daughter demanded to know if I had paid any money to her sister's rent before she would allow me to attend my granddaughter's birthday party. I learned later that she had decided to manipulate me into paying her for her custody battle, and she wanted leverage. I hadn't paid any rent, and I told her that. I was

invited to the party only to be uninvited a week later. I decided then that never again would I allow questions of this nature. My finances are my business and have nothing to do with her."

Setting Financial and Practical Boundaries

Financial boundaries are often the most challenging yet necessary to establish. You have the right to say no to financial requests, regardless of the circumstances your adult child presents. You can choose to help occasionally without creating an expectation of ongoing support. If you do provide assistance, you can attach reasonable conditions or timelines. Remember that repeatedly rescuing an adult child from the consequences of their choices often enables rather than helps them.

Similarly, you can set boundaries around practical help like babysitting, emergency childcare, or other favors. You might choose to help sometimes while making it clear that you're not available on demand. Your time and energy matter, and you deserve to be asked respectfully rather than expected to drop everything whenever needed.

> **The Secrecy Trap**
>
> When estranged children demand complete silence about family problems, ask yourself:
>
> ❖ Are they asking for reasonable privacy or enforced isolation?
> ❖ Do they extend the same courtesy by not discussing you with others?
> ❖ Are you being asked to protect them from the natural consequences of their choices?
> ❖ Would a neutral observer see their demands as fair?
>
> Remember: Healthy privacy protects everyone. Enforced secrecy typically protects the person creating the problems.

Communication Boundaries

Your adult child may attempt to control not just your interactions with them, but also who you talk to about your situation. Don't allow your child to control who you talk to when they refuse to even be in the conversation. This demand for secrecy serves their interests, not yours or the relationship's.

Michael's experience:

> *"My son told me I was 'seeking attention' by talking to my brother about our estrangement. He said if I really loved him, I'd keep our problems private. But I realized he was asking me to carry all this pain alone while he shared his version with anyone who would listen. I told him, 'I won't discuss intimate details inappropriately, but I won't be isolated in my grief either.'"*

While discretion and privacy are important—and you certainly shouldn't share intimate family details casually—you have the right to seek support from trusted friends, family members, or professionals. Abuse and manipulation thrive in darkness, not in light. Your adult child's insistence that you handle everything alone often stems from their awareness that objective observers would recognize unhealthy patterns.

This is why building those safe support systems we discussed earlier becomes so crucial. You need people who understand confidentiality, who won't gossip or interfere, but who can offer you perspective and emotional support. Professional counselors, trusted family members, or close friends who understand boundaries themselves can provide this vital support without compromising your family's privacy.

Electronic and Social Media Boundaries with Your Child

Just as you need electronic boundaries to protect yourself from extended family and acquaintances, you may need them with your adult child as well. Some estranged children respond to any outreach with cruel, hateful messages designed to wound. Others might contact you only to berate or blame you. You don't have to subject yourself to this treatment.

You can choose to limit communication to certain platforms, specific times, or particular topics. You might decide that you'll only respond to respectful communication, or that you need breaks from contact during particularly difficult periods. Some parents find it helpful to read messages when they're emotionally prepared rather than responding immediately to every text or email. This is where unfollowing, filters, email redirects, and even blocking become important.

If your adult child publicly attacks or humiliates you on social media, the boundaries you've established for online spaces apply here too. You can block, mute, or limit their access to your social media presence. Protecting your mental health isn't cruel—it's necessary for your ability to function and, ultimately, for any hope of future reconciliation.

When Contact Is Minimal or Hostile

Some estranged adult children maintain complete silence, while others make contact only to express anger, blame, or cruelty. In these situations, your boundaries may need to be more protective. You might choose to limit your availability for hostile communication, or to step back entirely for periods of time.

Remember that you can't control their choices, but you can control your responses. You don't have to accept abuse simply because it comes from your child. You can choose not to engage with manipulative communication, and you can prioritize your own emotional safety.

> **Red Flags That Signal Boundary Violations**
>
> Watch for these warning signs that your adult child is crossing healthy boundaries:
>
> ❖ Contacting you only when they need something.
> ❖ Threatening to withhold grandchildren if you don't comply with demands.
> ❖ Insisting you keep their treatment of you secret.
> ❖ Ignoring your stated limits.
> ❖ Treating you with cruelty when you are respectful.
> ❖ Using guilt, shame, or fear to manipulate your responses.
> ❖ Making demands without offering respect or reciprocity.

Boundaries That Protect Future Relationships

Healthy boundaries actually increase the chances of eventual reconciliation because they prevent the buildup of resentment and exhaustion that makes genuine forgiveness difficult. When you allow yourself to be consistently used or mistreated, you may find yourself growing increasingly bitter or emotionally depleted. This makes it harder to respond with love and openness if your child eventually wants to rebuild the relationship.

By maintaining your self-respect and emotional health, you preserve your capacity for authentic connection. You model healthy relationship dynamics, even if your child can't appreciate this now. And you ensure that if reconciliation does occur, it can be built on a foundation of mutual respect rather than a pattern of exploitation.

EXERCISE: Creating Your Boundary Statement

Write a clear, respectful boundary statement you can use when your adult child contacts you inappropriately. Use this template:

"I love you and want a relationship with you, but I need [specific behavior] to stop. I'm willing to [what you will do], but I won't [what you won't accept]. If you choose to [boundary violation], I will [your response]. This isn't about punishment—it's about creating space for us to interact respectfully."

_____

_____

_____

Practice saying this out loud until it feels natural. Remember, you're not asking permission—you're stating your reality.

Setting boundaries with your estranged adult child requires tremendous courage because it means accepting that you cannot control the outcome. You cannot boundary your way back into their life, and you cannot prevent them from choosing to distance themselves further. What you can do is create conditions that allow both of you to interact with dignity and respect.

These boundaries aren't about punishment or retaliation—they're about creating space for healing and growth. They protect you from further harm while leaving the door open for genuine reconciliation if and when your child is ready to engage respectfully.

Your adult child's estrangement is painful enough without allowing them to continue hurting you through manipulation, exploitation, or abuse. You deserve to be treated with basic human dignity, regardless of your relationship history. Setting boundaries honors both your worth and theirs, even if they cannot see it that way right now.

The Power of Self-Compassionate Boundaries

One of the most transformative—yet often overlooked—aspects of self-compassion is the ability to set and maintain healthy boundaries. While self-compassion is frequently associated with kindness and emotional warmth, it also involves courage—the courage to protect your well-being, even when it's uncomfortable. Remember that setting boundaries is not about building walls; it's about creating space for safety, healing, and growth.

True self-compassion means recognizing when something causes you harm and choosing not to expose yourself to unnecessary pain. It means honoring your needs without shame and understanding that you can remain open to connection and future reconciliation—even as you say "no" for now.

As you reflect on your journey, consider how your relationship with boundaries has evolved. Have there been moments when you've chosen peace over people-pleasing? Have you learned to say no without guilt, or to take space without self-recrimination? These are not selfish acts—they are self-honoring ones.

> **Compassionate Boundary Setting**
>
> Remember:
> - ❖ Boundaries protect, they don't punish.
> - ❖ You can be kind while being firm.
> - ❖ Your emotional safety matters
> - ❖ Limits can be temporary.
> - ❖ Flexibility doesn't mean weakness.
> - ❖ Self-protection is self-compassion.

Patricia shares her experience:

> *"Learning to set boundaries compassionately changed everything. Instead of feeling guilty for not attending family events where my son might be present, I could honor my need for emotional safety while still holding hope for future healing."*

Patricia's story is a reminder that setting boundaries doesn't close the door to love—it opens the door to self-respect. When you give yourself permission to protect your heart, you create the conditions for true compassion to flourish, not just for others, but for yourself.

Finding Balance in Daily Life

As parents begin to establish and strengthen their personal boundaries, they often find themselves reclaiming parts of life that were previously overshadowed by the pain of estrangement. Healthy boundaries aren't about shutting out love or giving up hope—they're about honoring your emotional well-being while making room for healing, growth, and meaningful experiences.

Moving toward acceptance doesn't mean the grief disappears. But by creating intentional boundaries—around conversations, expectations, time, or emotional availability—you can begin to hold your pain more gently, rather than letting it define every moment. Boundaries give you space to live *alongside* your sorrow, rather than *inside* it.

Patricia shares her experience:

> *"I started taking art classes—something I'd always wanted to do but never made time for. Some days I paint through tears, missing*

Signs of Growing Balance

You may be finding balance when you begin to:

- ❖ Set boundaries without constant self-doubt.
- ❖ Feel moments of joy, even while still holding grief.
- ❖ Make space for activities that nourish you.
- ❖ Allow conflicting emotions to coexist.
- ❖ Engage in daily life with more presence.
- ❖ Recognize that your well-being matters, too.
- ❖ Accept that healing can happen without resolution.

> *my son. Other days I lose myself in the creative process and feel genuinely happy. I'm learning both experiences can coexist."*

This is the quiet strength of boundaries: they help you carve out moments of peace and purpose, even when loss is still present. They allow you to engage with the world in a way that honors both your love and your limits.

As with everything on this path, there will be days of setback—moments when grief resurfaces sharply, or when holding a boundary feels more painful than letting it go. But over time, boundaries become a source of stability. They help anchor you through emotional waves, offering clarity and structure where there once was only uncertainty.

You are allowed to protect your heart and still hold space for hope. Boundaries don't mean the door is locked—they simply mean you're choosing when and how to open it, in ways that honor you.

As we conclude this exploration of boundaries, remember that navigating life during estrangement is not about achieving perfection—it's about developing sustainable practices that honor both your ongoing love for your adult child and your need for personal well-being.

Think of the journey ahead like tending a garden. Some days require careful pruning through boundary work, others call for nurturing new growth through connections and experiences. There will be seasons of challenge and seasons of bloom. The key is maintaining consistent care while accepting nature's timing.

As Linda discovered in that grocery store moment, each small success in maintaining healthy boundaries contributes to your overall healing. Every time you choose active hope over passive waiting, you strengthen your foundation for whatever lies ahead.

Moving Forward:

Take time to review the exercises and tools presented in this chapter. Choose one or two practices that resonate most strongly with you and commit to implementing them this week. Remember that building new patterns takes time—be patient with yourself as you develop these skills.

Key Takeaways:

- Your boundaries protect your capacity to heal and grow.
- You're not obligated to satisfy others' curiosity or defend your experience.
- You may need to set boundaries with your estranged adult child.
- Your primary responsibility is to protect your emotional well-being as you navigate this challenging journey.

In the next chapter, we'll explore how to write your new chapter, focusing on building a resilient future that honors both your past experiences and your potential for growth. Until then, hold gently to both your grief and your hope, knowing that each small step forward matters.

National Crisis Hotline

If you're experiencing thoughts of self-harm or feeling overwhelmed call:

988
or
1-800-273-8255

Available 24/7 for support and guidance.

Remember: Being honest about your struggles is a quiet form of bravery.

CHAPTER 8:

Acceptance and Hope—Letting Go without Giving Up

Throughout our journey together in previous chapters, we've explored the landscape of estrangement from multiple angles—understanding the complex dynamics at play, recognizing the profound grief that accompanies this loss, learning to navigate the shifting family relationships that emerge, and discovering ways to care for yourself in the midst of such pain. Each of these elements has been preparing you for perhaps the most challenging yet liberating step in this process: acceptance.

The boundary work we discussed, the self-care practices you've begun to implement, and the grief processing techniques you've learned have all been laying the groundwork for this moment. They've been teaching you that you can hold space for difficult emotions without being consumed by them, that you can love your adult child while also protecting your own well-being, and that healing can happen even when the relationship remains fractured. These skills haven't been separate lessons—they've been preparing you to embrace a different way of being with your estrangement.

The communication strategies we explored and the insights about family dynamics weren't just about potentially reconnecting with your adult child, though that hope remains precious. They were also about helping you understand that you have agency in how you respond to this situation, even when you cannot control the outcome. This agency, this power to choose your response, is at the heart of what acceptance offers.

Every tool we've discussed, from managing triggers to rebuilding your sense of identity beyond parenthood, has been guiding you toward this truth: you can acknowledge your reality without being defeated by it. You can grieve what you've lost while still nurturing hope for what might be possible. This is the essence of acceptance—not a passive surrender, but an active choice to work with your circumstances rather than against them.

Yet acceptance often gets misunderstood in the context of estrangement. Many parents worry that accepting their current situation means giving up hope or approving of their adult child's choices. Acknowledging reality as it is right now actually frees up energy for healing and growth.

Kylie Agllias notes:

> *"Acceptance in estrangement doesn't mean approval or resignation—it means acknowledging current reality while maintaining hope for future healing."*

Acceptance is acknowledging your current reality without condoning it. It involves recognizing the situation as it is, rather than constantly resisting or trying to rewrite it. This kind of acceptance releases the emotional struggle that often drains energy and replaces it with space for peace and perspective. It allows you to feel what you naturally feel—grief, confusion, even anger—without judgment, and it keeps the door open to future change, whether that comes gradually or suddenly.

What acceptance does *not* mean is

Understanding Acceptance

Acceptance Is:

- ❖ Acknowledging current reality.
- ❖ Releasing constant struggle.
- ❖ Creating space for peace.
- ❖ Allowing natural emotions.
- ❖ Staying open to change.

Acceptance Isn't:

- ❖ Approving of estrangement.
- ❖ Giving up hope.
- ❖ Denying pain.
- ❖ Forgetting the past.
- ❖ Closing off possibilities.

that you approve of the estrangement or agree with the choices your adult child has made. It doesn't mean giving up hope or pretending you're not in pain. Nor does it require you to forget what happened or to shut down emotionally to protect yourself. Acceptance simply invites you to stop fighting what is, so you can find steadiness in the midst of uncertainty.

Maria describes her journey with acceptance:

> *"I spent two years fighting reality—refusing to believe this was really happening, exhausting myself trying to force things to change. Learning to accept where things are right now doesn't mean I've given up. It means I can breathe again, live again, while still holding hope for the future."*

EXERCISE: Exploring Acceptance

Take a quiet moment to reflect:

- What aspects of your situation do you find hardest to accept?

  _____

  _____

  _____

- How much energy do you spend fighting current reality?

  _____

  _____

- What might become possible if you could accept things as they are right now?

- What fears come up when you think about acceptance?

- What small step toward acceptance feels possible today?

As parents move toward acceptance, they often discover new possibilities for finding joy and meaning in their lives. While the pain of estrangement isn't erased, the feelings are more manageable as they create space for other experiences.

Creating Space for Hope While Honoring Reality

Beyond simply setting boundaries, navigating social complexity, or accepting what cannot be changed, parents facing estrangement are often called to a more profound emotional task: cultivating a space where hope can coexist with truth. This kind of hope isn't rooted in fantasy or denial; rather, it allows for the possibility of reconciliation or healing without requiring it. It means recognizing the pain of what is, while still allowing room for what might one day be—without postponing one's own peace or well-being in the meantime.

Dr. Karl Pillemer explains:

> *"Hope in estrangement means staying open to possibility while building a meaningful life in the present."*

Thomas discovered this distinction through his own journey:

> *"For the first year, I confused hope with waiting. I put my life on hold, thinking any day my son would return. Learning to hope differently—to believe in possibility while living fully now—changed everything."*

This shift from passive waiting to active hoping requires developing emotional flexibility. It's the ability to hold seemingly contradictory experiences: feeling deep sadness about the estrangement while also finding joy in new experiences, missing your child intensely while building meaningful connections with others.

This approach often feels counter-intuitive at first. Many parents worry that creating a satisfying life somehow betrays their estranged child or signals they've given up on reconciliation. But choosing to live fully isn't a betrayal—it's an act of resilience. Building a meaningful, grounded life doesn't close the door to reconciliation; it often makes genuine connection more possible. When parents remain stuck in grief or suspend their own healing in the hope of reunion, they can unknowingly project an energy of urgency or emotional need that places strain on fragile relationships. In contrast, when parents prioritize their own wholeness, they bring steadiness, self-respect, and emotional clarity to any future contact.

Dr. Joshua Coleman writes:

> *"Creating a meaningful life during estrangement isn't betrayal—it's essential for both personal healing and potential reconciliation."*

Active Hope vs. Passive Waiting

Active Hope:

- Lives fully in the present.
- Creates new meaning.
- Builds connections.
- Takes healthy risks.
- Maintains boundaries.
- Allows for uncertainty.

Passive Waiting:

- Puts life on hold.
- Dwells in past.
- Isolates self.
- Avoids change.
- Ignores needs.
- Demands certainty.

EXERCISE: Expanding Your Life Space

Take a moment to consider:

- What activities or interests have you set aside?

  _____

  _____

  _____

- What new experiences appeal to you?

  _____

  _____

  _____

- What relationships could use attention?

  _____

  _____

  _____

- What goals feel meaningful now?

  _____

  _____

  _____

- What small step could you take this week?

_____

_____

_____

Start with one small action that moves you toward fuller living while honoring your ongoing love for your estranged child.

Building New Connections

One of the most healing aspects of moving forward involves developing new relationships and strengthening existing ones. However, this often requires overcoming fears about vulnerability and trust.

Sarah describes her initial reluctance:

> *"After my daughter cut contact, I was terrified of getting close to anyone. What if they rejected me too? But slowly, I started opening up to select people. Now I have deeper friendships than ever before—people who know my whole story and still choose to be in my life."*

EXERCISE: Connection Inventory

List your current relationships in three categories below.

For each category, consider:

- What these relationships offer you
- How you can nurture them
- What boundaries you need

- Ways to deepen connection
- Potential risks and rewards

Inner Circle:

Those who fully understand and support your journey.

_____

_____

_____

Middle Circle:

Casual friends and acquaintances who offer normal social connection.

_____

_____

_____

Outer Circle:

New or potential connections you'd like to develop.

_____

_____

_____

Remember: Building new connections takes time and doesn't betray your love for your estranged child. You're expanding your heart, not replacing anyone.

Creating New Meanings

One powerful way to maintain healthy hope involves creating new meanings from difficult experiences. This allows your pain to be part of a larger, evolving story. When parents find ways to transform suffering into something purposeful, it can restore a sense of agency and reconnect them to what matters most. Whether it's sharing hard-won wisdom, supporting others through similar struggles, or expressing the journey through art or advocacy, meaning-making becomes a quiet rebellion against despair. It says: "This experience shaped me, but it doesn't define me." It can also open unexpected paths to healing—not only within, but sometimes with the estranged child as well.

> **Finding Meaning in Challenge**
>
> Consider ways to:
> ❖ Share your wisdom.
> ❖ Support others.
> ❖ Create beauty.
> ❖ Build community.
> ❖ Learn new skills.
> ❖ Honor your journey.

Patricia discovered this through volunteer work:

> "Using my experience to help other parents navigate estrangement gave purpose to my pain. It doesn't erase the hurt, but it helps me feel like something positive can come from this challenge."

Finding meaning creates additional spaces in your heart and life where hope and healing can grow.

Building Resilient Hope

Maintaining hope through long-term estrangement isn't about blind optimism—it's about developing sustainable hope, the kind that can endure uncertainty and pain without collapsing. This kind of hope isn't passive; it's active, intentional, and rooted in both emotional resilience and practical strategies.

Sustainable hope requires cultivating tools and skills that help parents weather the ongoing emotional turbulence of estrangement—grief, anger, uncertainty, and longing—while still remaining open to future possibility. This is what we call hope resilience: the ability to hold space for what might be, even when the present offers little reassurance. It means finding ways to stay grounded in reality without letting go of the belief that healing, growth, or connection may still unfold over time.

As with other themes we've explored in this book, building a "hope kit" can be a grounding and empowering exercise. At this stage in your journey, your hope kit may stand on its own or naturally evolve from—or integrate with—other emotional support kits you've already created. It becomes a personalized collection of tools, reminders, and practices that help you reconnect with possibility, especially during moments when hope feels distant or fragile.

Linda describes her approach:

> *"I keep what I call my 'hope kit'—tangible reminders that change is possible and that I'm growing stronger through this challenge. On hard days, these simple objects help me maintain perspective without falling into either denial or despair."*

EXERCISE: Creating Your Hope Kit

Gather items that represent:

- Personal growth
- Meaningful connections
- New experiences
- Inner strength
- Future possibilities
- Present gratitude

Include practical tools like:

- Inspiration cards
- Comfort objects

- Photos of happy moments
- Journal for reflection
- Crisis contact numbers
- Self-care supplies

Remember: This kit supports your journey but doesn't deny its difficulty. It's about maintaining balance while navigating uncertainty.

Sustainable hope grows through small, consistent actions rather than dramatic gestures. These quiet practices build inner strength over time, helping you stay connected to what matters most without losing yourself in longing. You might light a candle and spend five minutes holding both your love for your child and your commitment to living fully now—allowing both truths to coexist without needing resolution in that moment.

You could also try writing a short note to yourself each morning—something compassionate and grounding, like "I can hold space for healing without putting my life on hold." Or keep a small object on your nightstand that symbolizes resilience: a stone from a meaningful place, a photo of yourself at a time you felt strong, or a written quote that affirms your path.

Hope-Sustaining Practices

Morning:
Set intention for balanced living.

Evening:
Acknowledge both challenges and gifts.

Weekly:
Review growth and learning.

Monthly:
Adjust and renew practices.

As needed:
Connect with support.

These simple, nourishing rituals help you begin each day with gentle hope rather than desperate waiting—creating a rhythm of care that sustains you no matter where your journey leads.

Dr. Karl Pillemer emphasizes:

> *"Daily rituals that acknowledge both loss and growth help parents maintain emotional balance during extended periods of estrangement."*

Creating Your Hopeful Path Forward

As we deepen our exploration of acceptance and hope, it's important to recognize that healing from estrangement isn't a linear journey.

Margaret shares her insight:

> *"Some days I feel strong and centered, others I'm knocked sideways by a simple memory. Learning to navigate these ups and downs while maintaining healthy boundaries has been crucial for my long-term well-being."*

Think of resilience as something you build, much like a muscle—it doesn't appear overnight, but grows through steady practice and repeated engagement with life's challenges. Every time you maintain a boundary with grace, respond to a trigger with self-compassion, or choose active hope instead of slipping into passive waiting, you're doing the quiet, powerful work of strengthening your emotional core. Over time, these choices build your capacity to cope in healthy, grounded ways—even when circumstances remain uncertain or painful. Resilience isn't about never feeling hurt; it's about developing the inner flexibility and strength to keep going with integrity and care for yourself.

Every parent's journey through estrangement is unique, requiring personalized strategies that reflect their specific circumstances and needs.

Thomas describes how he developed his approach:

> *"I realized I needed different tools for different situations—something quick for unexpected encounters, deeper practices for planned events, and emergency strategies for particularly difficult days."*

Next, we'll explore how to write your new chapter, focusing on building a resilient future that honors both your past experiences and your potential for growth. Until then, hold gently to both your grief and your hope, knowing that each small step forward matters.

> ### National Crisis Hotline
>
> If you're experiencing thoughts of self-harm or feeling overwhelmed call:
>
> **988**
> **or**
> **1-800-273-8255**
>
> Available 24/7 for support and guidance.
>
> Remember: Asking for help shows courage and emotional intelligence.

CHAPTER 9:

Writing Your New Chapter—Reclaiming Joy and Building a Resilient Future

Janet sits in her newly organized art studio, surrounded by colorful canvases and the gentle morning light. Three years ago, when her daughter stopped speaking to her, she could never have imagined finding joy again. But here she is, preparing to teach her first painting class to other parents navigating estrangement. "Sometimes," she reflects, "the story we think is ending becomes the beginning of something we never expected."

This transformation didn't happen overnight. Like many parents experiencing estrangement, Janet's journey began in survival mode—simply getting through each day, managing boundaries, and practicing self-compassion as we discussed in previous chapters. But gradually, something shifted. She discovered that while the pain of estrangement remained, it didn't have to define her entire existence.

As Dr. Joshua Coleman notes in his work with estranged parents:

> *"The goal isn't to get rid of the pain of the estrangement, but to reduce its power to organize your life around it."*

This realization often marks a crucial turning point—the moment when parents begin moving from merely surviving to actively creating their future. It's like opening a new chapter in a book that seemed to have stopped mid-sentence. The previous chapters don't disappear, but new possibilities begin to emerge.

Understanding Resilience in Estrangement

When dealing with estrangement from an adult child, resilience isn't just toughening up or shutting down emotionally. Instead of becoming cold or numb, it's about learning to stay emotionally open and vulnerable to life, even while carrying deep pain or grief. True resilience here doesn't only mean strength; it also means softness and compassion towards yourself. It's a balance of being strong enough to keep going but gentle enough to let yourself experience loss without breaking.

Thomas discovered this truth through an unexpected metaphor:

> **Signs of Growing Resilience**
>
> You may notice:
> - Quicker recovery from triggers.
> - More balanced emotional responses.
> - Increased openness to new experiences.
> - Greater ability to hold hope and pain together.
> - More consistent self-care practices.
> - Deeper connections with others.

> "My therapist compared resilience to a tree bending in a storm. The wind doesn't stop blowing just because we wish it would, but we can develop the flexibility to bend without breaking. Some days the wind is stronger than others, but the roots grow deeper with each challenge."

Creating Physical Space for New Beginnings

Healing from estrangement requires more than time—it calls for a reorganization of your inner and outer life, a willingness to see old patterns in new ways, and the courage to create space for growth, joy, and meaning that is not dependent on reconciliation. It means finding ways to reconnect with your own sense of purpose, even as you carry the weight of loss.

Margaret shares how she started rebuilding:

> *"For months, my craft room sat untouched—it was where I used to make quilts for my grandchildren. One day, I realized I could either let that space collect dust or transform it into something new. I decided to teach quilting to women in my neighborhood. Now it's become a place of healing for all of us."*

Moments like these don't erase the pain, but they shift the focus from what's missing to what's still possible. When parents take small steps toward creativity, service, or connection, they begin to reshape not just their routines, but their identity—no longer defined solely by estrangement, but by resilience, contribution, and personal meaning.

This process of reclaiming and transforming spaces, activities, and dreams represents a crucial step in building resilience. When parents begin actively creating new meaning in their lives, they often discover strengths and possibilities they never knew they had.

EXERCISE: Space and Place Inventory

Take a gentle look around your life:

- Which spaces feel heavy with loss?

    _____

    _____

    _____

- What activities have you stopped enjoying?

    _____

    _____

    _____

- Which dreams feel on hold?

  _____

  _____

  _____

- Where might transformation be possible?

  _____

  _____

  _____

- What small changes feel manageable now?

  _____

  _____

  _____

Remember: Start small. Choose one space or activity to begin with rather than trying to transform everything at once.

Finding Purpose Beyond Pain

Estrangement may alter the relationship you have with your child, but it doesn't erase your identity as a parent—or your capacity to care, give, and grow. The love you carry doesn't vanish; it simply needs a new place to land. Finding purpose beyond the pain of estrangement means learning to channel that deep well of love, patience, and strength into something life-giving. Whether through creative expression, acts of service, spiritual growth, or community engagement, expanding your sense of purpose creates room for healing. It helps you honor your role as a parent while reclaiming agency in a situation that often feels beyond your control.

Linda discovered her new direction through writing:

> *"I started journaling to process my grief, but it evolved into something more. Now I lead writing workshops for parents navigating family challenges. My pain became a bridge to helping others, and that gives it meaning beyond just hurting."*

Exploring New Purpose

Consider areas like:
- Creative expression
- Supporting others
- Learning new skills
- Community service
- Personal growth
- Professional development
- Relationship building

Miriam found unexpected healing through connection:

> *"I used to cry every Mother's Day thinking of my daughter—what I said, what I didn't say, how silence grew between us. Then a young woman at my church lost her mom, and I felt this pull to reach out to her. We started meeting for coffee, and we became close. I still pray for my daughter every day but mentoring someone who needs a mother's care gives me new purpose and a way to share my love. It's not the same, but it's something very special."*

Sarah shares her experience:

> *"Missing my grandchildren felt like carrying a quiet ache every day. But as I worked through my grief and slowly began to heal, I found myself drawn to volunteering at a local school, helping young children learn to read. I didn't realize how much it would mean to me. Being there—offering encouragement, watching their confidence grow—healed a part of my heart I thought would always stay broken."*

Julie found excitement and friendship in traveling:

> *"After my adult children became estranged, I felt isolated and unsure how to fill the emptiness. Then, by chance, I met some local women who were near my own age. We started meeting for coffee, and soon those gatherings turned into weekend trips—exploring nearby towns, hiking trails, and museums. These shared experiences brought laughter and connection back into my life. Through this new circle of friendship, I rediscovered joy and a sense of belonging."*

Expanding your sense of purpose doesn't mean giving up on love or hope—it means taking back some control in a situation that often feels powerless. By finding meaning in things like creativity, community, helping others, or growing as a person, you create space to heal. In that space, love can still exist—calmer, more stable, and not tied to whether things ever change.

Finding Joy

The concept of joy often feels foreign or even inappropriate to parents experiencing estrangement. Many parents need permission to experience joy again. They often fear that feeling happy means they're accepting or approving of the estrangement. In reality, building capacity for joy creates emotional resilience that better serves everyone—including the estranged adult child, should reconciliation occur.

Sarah remembers her initial resistance:

> *"I felt guilty about any moment of happiness, like I was betraying my love for my son by not being constantly sad. Learning to allow joy back into my life was itself a journey."*

Feeling happy doesn't mean you are letting go of your child or condoning the painful separation. This belief traps parents in ongoing grief and guilt, as if being unhappy proves their love. But this way of thinking mixes up suffering with devotion. The cultural narrative that equates love with constant worry and pain is particularly damaging for estranged parents, who may feel that any joy they experience represents a failure of their parental duty.

This myth of perpetual sorrow often stems from well-meaning but misguided sources. Friends might comment, "I don't know how you can smile when your child won't speak to you," or family members might interpret moments of lightness as evidence that "you're getting over it." These external pressures compound the internal guilt parents already feel, creating a prison of enforced misery.

Sheri McGregor, therapist and author, explains:

> *"Parents often feel stuck in their pain, as though moving forward would somehow diminish their love for their child. But allowing yourself to experience joy isn't betraying your child—it's an act of emotional survival."*

The truth is that the more we practice resilience, the stronger we become. Finding moments of joy and healing doesn't mean giving up on reconciliation or forgetting the pain—it means building emotional strength. Remember, as we've discussed previously: parents who learn to be kind to themselves and feel happiness again are actually better prepared to handle a possible reunion.

The irony is that by releasing themselves from the prison of constant sorrow, parents often become more ready for the very thing they hope for most: a renewed relationship with their child built on a foundation of emotional health rather than desperation or guilt. Consider the difference between these two scenarios:

A parent who has remained locked in grief approaches a potential reconciliation from a place of emotional depletion. Their need for connection may feel overwhelming to an adult child who is still processing their own healing journey. The parent's pain, while genuine, can inadvertently place pressure on the relationship before it has a chance to rebuild.

In contrast, a parent who has done the work of rebuilding their capacity for joy approaches reconciliation from a place of emotional wholeness. They can offer presence without desperation, love without conditions, and engagement without the weight of accumulated suffering. This creates space for authentic connection to emerge naturally.

Love is not a finite resource that must be hoarded in the form of suffering. The capacity to feel joy doesn't deplete your love for your child—it enriches it. When you allow yourself to experience happiness, you're not abandoning your child; you're modeling emotional resilience and showing that healing is possible. This modeling can be particularly powerful if reconciliation does occur, as it demonstrates that relationships can survive difficulty and that individuals can grow through adversity.

The Ripple Effect of Joy

When parents begin to reclaim joy, the effects extend far beyond their own emotional well-being. Partners who have watched their loved one suffer may feel relief and renewed hope. Other family members, who may have been walking on eggshells or feeling helpless, can begin to relax. The entire family system begins to shift toward health rather than organizing around the crisis of estrangement.

Emily, who watched her mother deal with the estrangement from her older sister, shares this experience:

> *"For years, I saw my mom disappear into her grief for my sister. It felt like we all lived in the shadow of that silence. But lately, she's laughing again—we started taking walks, cooking new recipes together, and I can feel her coming back to life. I didn't realize how much I missed her until I saw that spark return."*

This personal healing often radiates outward into the broader community. When a parent begins volunteering, joining a local book club, or simply showing up more fully in daily life, neighbors and strangers alike feel the benefit. A single act of kindness, a shared laugh, or a consistent presence in a community group can create ripples of connection. In this way, reclaiming joy isn't just a private act of healing—it becomes a public act

---

Community Building Pathways

Consider exploring:
- ❖ Volunteer opportunities
- ❖ Interest-based groups
- ❖ Learning communities
- ❖ Support circles
- ❖ Creative collectives
- ❖ Service organizations

of contribution, offering hope and warmth to others who may also be quietly carrying pain.

Thomas found his community through an unexpected avenue:

> *"I joined a community garden, mainly to get out of the house. Gradually, I realized I was building relationships with people who shared my interest in growing things. We rarely talk about our personal struggles directly, but there's something healing about nurturing plants alongside others who understand that growth takes time."*

This shift doesn't happen overnight, and it's not always linear. There will be moments when guilt returns, when joy feels inappropriate, when the weight of loss overshadows any glimmer of happiness. These setbacks are normal and expected. The goal isn't to eliminate all sadness but to create space for a fuller range of emotions.

Starting Small: The Micro-Moments of Joy

Joy doesn't have to arrive as a dramatic breakthrough. Often, it begins as tiny pinpricks of light in the darkness—a moment of laughter at a friend's joke, the pleasure of a perfectly brewed cup of coffee, the satisfaction of completing a small task. These micro-moments of joy are not insignificant; they are the building blocks of emotional recovery. Celebrate these moments.

Some parents find it helpful to think of joy as a skill that requires practice. Just as physical therapy gradually rebuilds strength after an injury, emotional

> **Permission Statements**
>
> Create personal permission statements that you can return to when guilt about joy arises:
>
> "I give myself permission to feel happiness without it meaning I love my child less."
>
> "Joy is not betrayal; it is healing."
>
> "I can hold both love for my child and care for myself."
>
> "My emotional well-being serves everyone, including my estranged child."
>
> "I am worthy of happiness, regardless of my parenting outcomes."

healing gradually rebuilds capacity for happiness. Starting small prevents overwhelm and allows parents to build tolerance for positive emotions without triggering intense guilt.

EXERCISE: Joy Inventory

- Remember: What brought you joy before estrangement?

    _____

    _____

- Notice: What small pleasures still peek through?

    _____

    _____

- Imagine: What new experiences appeal to you?

    _____

    _____

- Consider: Who helps you feel lighter?

    _____

- Explore: What activities spark your interest?

    _____

    _____

> Start with tiny moments of joy—a cup of tea in the morning sun, a favorite song, a walk in nature. These small pleasures build the foundation for larger happiness without overwhelming your grief or triggering guilt.

In Chapter 4, we explored how journaling can support the healing process. In a similar way, keeping a simple record of moments when you feel even brief glimmers of joy, contentment, or peace can gently expand your capacity to experience more of them. This isn't about forced positivity or ignoring pain—it's about learning to notice the full spectrum of your emotional experience. By intentionally acknowledging moments of light, no matter how small, you begin to shift your focus from surviving to also allowing space for living.

EXERCISE: The Joy Journal

Note:

- What was happening when you felt the positive emotion?
- How long did it last?
- What, if anything, interrupted it?
- How did your body feel?
- What thoughts accompanied the feeling?

Over time, patterns may emerge that help you understand your unique pathways to joy and healing.

Reclaiming joy is not a destination but a practice. There will be days when happiness feels impossible, when the weight of loss overshadows everything else. These days are part of the journey, not evidence of failure. The goal is to gradually expand your capacity for the full range of human emotion, creating space for both grief and joy to coexist.

Remember that your healing journey is not separate from your love for your child—it is an expression of it. By choosing to rebuild your capacity for joy, you honor both your own life and the hope for future connection. You demonstrate that love can survive difficulty, that people can grow through adversity, and that healing is always possible, even in the most painful circumstances.

Resilience: Surviving to Thriving

The journey from survival estrangement to thriving requires both courage and practical tools. Again, resilience isn't about "toughening up" but rather developing flexibility and strength while maintaining sensitivity. As with the other subjects we've discussed, building emotional resilience happens through small, consistent actions rather than dramatic gestures. Be sure to choose practices that feel natural and sustainable for you.

Thomas shares how this perspective shifted his approach:

> **Simple Resilience Builders**
>
> Daily practices might include:
>
> ❖ Brief meditation or breathing exercises
> ❖ Gentle physical movement
> ❖ Gratitude moments
> ❖ Connection with supportive people
> ❖ Creative expression
> ❖ Nature time
> ❖ Acts of service

> *"I used to think being strong meant not feeling the pain anymore. Now I understand that true strength is being able to feel everything—the grief, the love, the hope, the disappointment—without being overwhelmed by any of it."*

Physical Wellness as Emotional Support

When we're going through difficult emotional periods, the state of our physical well-being plays a powerful role in how we cope. The body and mind are deeply connected, and when emotional strain weighs heavily on us, tending to our physical routines can provide a much-needed sense of stability. Consistent rest, balanced eating habits, and even light physical activity can quietly strengthen our inner resilience, giving us more bandwidth to manage what we're feeling.

Often, the simplest physical habits serve as anchors during times of emotional turbulence. Prioritizing calm movement, fueling ourselves with steady nourishment, and maintaining a rhythm of rest can reinforce the foundation we need to process and recover from internal struggles. These acts may seem small, but they work in tandem to support emotional clarity and endurance, making it easier to navigate through complex or overwhelming experiences.

Margaret found this connection particularly powerful:

> *"I started walking every morning, not for exercise really, but just to move and breathe. Something about being in motion helps me process emotions that feel stuck when I'm sitting still. And on days when grief feels heavy, just getting outside and moving reminds me that I'm still part of the living world."*

EXERCISE: Physical Resilience Check-In

Take a gentle inventory of:

- Your sleep patterns
- Eating habits
- Physical movement
- Stress levels
- Energy throughout the day

_____

_____

_____

_____

_____

_____

_____

_____

Choose one small area to focus on improving this week. Remember, the goal isn't perfection but rather supporting your emotional well-being through physical care.

Creating New Traditions

One of the most emotionally complex challenges for parents experiencing estrangement is navigating holidays and special occasions. These times are traditionally centered around family, connection, and shared memories—so their arrival can intensify feelings of loss, longing, and loneliness.

Many parents discover, through the journey of healing, that an advanced form of self-compassion involves more than just soothing their pain. It invites them to create new meanings and traditions, ones that gently acknowledge the absence of a loved one while also making space for hope, presence, and joy. This isn't about forgetting the past—it's about honoring it while refusing to stay frozen within it.

Psychologist Pauline Boss emphasizes that resilience isn't about "getting over" a loss but learning to live with uncertainty:

> "The goal is to build both/and thinking—the ability to hold two opposing ideas in your mind at the same time."

These both/and celebrations can take many forms. For some, it might mean hosting a "friendsgiving" with neighbors or chosen family. For others, it may be volunteering at a local shelter, traveling to a new place, or spending the day in nature. This is not an either/or decision.

It is both/and: both grief and celebration, both remembrance and renewal.

In contrast, trying to maintain old traditions unchanged can sometimes intensify the pain, especially if they no longer reflect your current reality. Instead, consider designing new rituals that acknowledge your grief while also tending to your deep human need for connection—to yourself, to others, and to life.

New traditions can be as grand or as simple as needed. The key is intentionality: creating space not only for grief, but also for life beyond it. A quiet breakfast in nature, an annual personal retreat, or a themed dinner with others who understand—each becomes an act of self-compassion and quiet defiance against the narrative that a parent's joy must end when the relationship with a child fractures.

There is no "moving on," only moving forward—carrying both the weight of loss and the hope for healing. And with time, these new traditions can become anchors: not replacements for what was lost, but testaments to what endures.

Linda shares how she transformed her approach to Christmas:

> "Instead of sitting home alone feeling sad about missing family celebrations, I started hosting a dinner for other parents in similar situations. We call it our 'Chosen Family Feast.' Yes, there are tears sometimes, but there's also laughter and understanding. We're creating something new from our shared experience."

Building New Traditions

Consider creating:

❖ Weekly routines that nurture you.
❖ Monthly activities that challenge growth.
❖ Seasonal celebrations that honor change.
❖ Annual rituals that mark progress.
❖ Personal ceremonies for processing grief.
❖ Flexible traditions that can evolve.
❖ Community connections that offer support.

Remember: You're not replacing what was lost; you're layering new meaning onto your story, one intentional choice at a time.

This process is not always easy, but it is deeply empowering. In choosing to shape your own narrative—one that includes joy, agency, and meaning—you reclaim a sense of dignity and direction. Creating new traditions becomes a quiet but powerful way of saying: "I matter. My experience matters. I can find beauty, even here."

You are not erasing the past. You are building a bridge between what was and what is becoming.

EXERCISE: Tradition Transformation

Choose an upcoming holiday or special occasion:

_____

1. Acknowledge what you miss about old traditions:

   _____

   _____

   _____

2. Identify what you need now:

   - Connection
   - Meaning
   - Joy
   - Peace
   - Understanding

   _____

   _____

   _____

3. Brainstorm new possibilities that meet these needs:

   _____

   _____

   _____

4. Start small—perhaps one new element this year:

   _____

   _____

5. Include others who understand and support your journey:

   _____

   _____

Professional Development and Personal Growth

Many parents of estranged adult children find that focusing on professional growth or personal development becomes a vital way to cope during this painful time. The absence of their child can feel overwhelming, but shifting attention to career goals, skill-building, or meaningful work can offer both a helpful distraction and a real sense of purpose. Whether it's aiming for a promotion, learning new tools, or taking on tough projects, investing in

Growth Opportunities

Consider exploring:

❖ Educational programs
❖ Career development
❖ New skills acquisition
❖ Professional certifications
❖ Creative workshops
❖ Personal enrichment courses

work provides structure and progress, which can ease feelings of helplessness or being stuck.

Personal growth can be just as powerful. With unexpected time and emotional space, many parents return to interests they once set aside—like going back to school, exploring creative hobbies, committing to fitness, or deepening spiritual practices. Learning something new or working toward a goal can create forward momentum, a sharp contrast to the sense of stagnation estrangement often brings. These pursuits can also open doors to new social connections and community, which are especially important when family bonds are strained.

The benefits go beyond keeping busy. Reaching goals—whether professional or personal—helps rebuild confidence and self-worth, which may have been shaken by the family crisis. It also helps parents reconnect with parts of their identity beyond being a parent, reminding them of their strengths and value in other areas of life. This renewed sense of purpose doesn't lessen their love for their child or their hope for reconciliation, but it gives them a stronger foundation of self-respect and emotional balance as they face the challenges of estrangement.

Margaret describes her journey:

> *"I went back to school to finish my degree—something I'd put off for years. Focusing on learning helped me feel like I was moving forward instead of just waiting for things to change with my daughter. Now I have new goals and achievements that belong to me, regardless of what happens with our relationship."*

Planning for Your Future: Creating Vision with Flexibility

As we continue exploring how to build a resilient future, it's important to acknowledge the delicate balance between making meaningful plans and staying open to life's uncertainties. For many parents, this can feel like a painful tug-of-war. There's often a quiet fear that moving forward—whether by pursuing a new goal, taking a trip, or making a big decision—somehow means abandoning hope for reconciliation. The worry is that embracing life might signal indifference, or that joy and purpose can only return after things are repaired.

But in truth, creating a meaningful life doesn't close the door on reconciliation—it builds a stronger, more grounded foundation for it. Living fully and intentionally strengthens your emotional resilience, broadens your support network, and helps you feel more whole. And from that place of strength, you are better able to show up with clarity, compassion, and openness—should a path to reconnection ever emerge.

Sarah discovered this truth through her own experience:

> *"For two years, I put everything on hold—travel, career changes, even home improvements. I thought making plans meant accepting the estrangement was permanent. My therapist helped me see that building a life worth living isn't about closing doors; it's about opening new ones while keeping my heart open to all possibilities."*

Creating Your Vision

The process of envisioning your future begins with giving yourself permission to dream again. Again, this doesn't mean forgetting your estranged child or abandoning hope for reconciliation. Instead, it means acknowledging that your life can hold both ongoing love for your child and new sources of meaning and purpose.

EXERCISE: Permission to Dream

Find a quiet moment and gentle space to explore:

1. What would you do if you knew it was okay to move forward?

_____

_____

2. Which dreams did you set aside that still call to you?

_____

_____

3. What new interests have emerged during your healing journey?

_____

_____

4. Where do you feel drawn to contribute or connect?

_____

_____

5. What would "thriving" look like while holding space for both grief and growth?

_____

_____

_____

Remember: Your dreams don't replace your love for your child; they expand your capacity for living fully.

Building Flexible Plans

Creating plans with built-in flexibility allows parents of estranged adult children to maintain forward momentum without feeling like they're abandoning hope. Estrangement brings a level of unpredictability that can make long-term planning feel risky or even emotionally disloyal. But rather than avoiding plans altogether, the key is to design them with enough give—like a house with doors that open in multiple directions, or a bridge with joints that can bend without breaking.

Flexible planning acknowledges reality while still making space for growth, joy, and unexpected turns. It means allowing yourself to invest in your future without requiring certainty about how your family story will unfold. This approach can reduce anxiety and create a sense of empowerment, even in the face of ongoing ambiguity.

> **Vision Building Blocks**
>
> Consider exploring:
>
> ❖ Personal growth goals
> ❖ Creative pursuits
> ❖ Professional development
> ❖ Community involvement
> ❖ Travel adventures
> ❖ Learning opportunities
> ❖ Relationship building
> ❖ Legacy creation

Angela shares how she began to shift her approach:

> *"For a long time, I avoided planning anything more than a week out. I was afraid that if I took a trip or committed to a new job, my daughter might call—and I'd miss my chance to reconnect. But the waiting wore me down.*

Eventually, I made a plan to spend a month in a coastal town I'd always loved. I told myself, If she reaches out, I can come back early. If not, I'll still be somewhere that nourishes me. She didn't call—but I came home with a clearer mind, new friends, and a deeper sense that my life is still mine to live."

Angela didn't give up on hope. She simply created a plan that could stretch if needed—and that still served her well, even as it was.

Creating Your Support Network

Building a resilient future means continually tending to your support system. While we explored this earlier in the book, it's worth revisiting as your needs evolve. As you heal from estrangement and begin shaping a new future, take time to reassess who is in your support circle. The people who helped you survive the initial shock may not be the same ones who can walk with you through this next phase.

For example, in the early days of my estrangement from my daughter, online support groups were a lifeline—I needed people who understood that specific pain. Now, my focus has shifted toward strengthening my existing family ties and cultivating new, more life-affirming connections. Support isn't static. It grows with you.

Margaret shares her experience:

> *"I realized I needed different kinds of support—practical help, emotional understanding, professional guidance, and simple friendship. Building this network took time, but it's become my foundation for moving forward."*

The key is finding connections that feel authentic and supportive without pressure to share more than feels comfortable.

EXERCISE: Support Network

Identify gaps in your support system and consider ways to fill them through:

- Support groups
- Professional relationships
- Community involvement
- Friendship development
- Family connections
- Online communities

_____

_____

_____

_____

_____

_____

_____

_____

_____

Embracing Your Continuing Story

A resilient future isn't about forgetting or leaping into reinvention overnight. It isn't always dramatic or sweeping. More often, it grows in quiet moments of choice—small, consistent actions that slowly but surely create new rhythms, new meaning, and new ways of being.

As we continue our journey, let's return to Janet in her art studio:

> "The canvases I paint now are different from what I would have created before the estrangement," she reflects. "They hold both shadow and light, pain and beauty. Just like my life."

In her words—and in her art—we glimpse the quiet courage it takes to integrate the past rather than erase it. Her brushstrokes don't deny the sorrow, but neither do they let it define the whole. She allows herself to feel everything and, in doing so, creates something new. This image of beauty born from both darkness and light speaks to the heart of resilience: the capacity to carry our grief without being consumed by it, and to shape meaning from even the most fractured experiences.

Thomas understands this well:

> *"I started with just one small change. I took a different route to work—one that didn't pass my son's old school. It wasn't easy at first. I missed the familiar, even though it hurt. But that one choice led to another. I stopped at a new coffee shop. I met a few other early morning regulars. There was one guy who always read poetry at the counter, and we started talking. Gradually, without even realizing it, I built a morning routine that didn't just avoid pain—it nurtured me. Small steps. That's all it was. But they added up. They still do."*

Janet and Thomas remind us that healing doesn't demand perfection. It asks only for presence, and the willingness to try again—one canvas, one route, one conversation at a time.

Reconciliation

As I said in the chapter A Mother's Journey, this book is not a roadmap to reconciliation, but a pathway to joy regardless of what might happen in the future. Still, the hope of reconnection lingers quietly alongside the grief. It may never come. Or it may arrive unexpectedly, shaped by time, maturity, or healing on both sides.

You don't have to chase or force reconciliation. In fact, stepping back can sometimes create the space where growth becomes possible. Letting go of control is not the same as giving up—it's an act of deep respect for your own well-being and for the agency of your adult child.

If reconciliation is ever to happen, it will be because both parties are ready to meet again—not in the past, but in a new, healthier present. Until then, you are still allowed to live fully, love deeply, and heal profoundly.

You don't need to wait for someone else's change in order to change your own life. Any future reconciliation must be built on a foundation of truth, mutual respect, and personal boundaries—not fantasy or guilt. Meanwhile, hope can live quietly in the background, like a candle you don't have to stare at constantly.

Whether or not your relationship is ever restored, your healing matters. Your life, your peace, and your joy are not on hold. Remember that you can hold more than one thing in your heart. One of those things should be joy.

Moving Forward with Hope and Resilience

Writing your next chapter is not a one-time act—it's a living, evolving process. Some days may feel full of clarity and peace, while others may stir grief, doubt, or longing. This ebb and flow is not a sign of failure; it's a natural part of healing and growth.

True resilience doesn't mean feeling strong every moment—it means honoring your experiences, responding with self-compassion, and continuing to move forward, even when the path is uncertain.

A grounded and hopeful future rests on deep self-understanding, honest connection, and the quiet courage to keep going. You are not defined by what has happened, but by how you choose to meet each new day.

Your story is still unfolding. And you have the strength, the wisdom, and the grace to shape it with intention and hope.

Keys Takeaways:

- Experiencing happiness doesn't diminish your love for your estranged child
- Finding joy in the present moment strengthens your capacity for connection and keeps your heart open to future possibilities, including reconciliation
- You are allowed to build a life filled with love, purpose, and joy—not as a replacement for what was lost, but as a foundation for healing, growth, and hope.
- Sustainable hope is built through small, consistent actions that honor both your grief and your resilience

In the next chapter, we'll explore estate planning and legacy decisions through the lens of estrangement. Approaching these matters with both clarity and flexibility can bring a deep sense of peace and empower you to move forward with greater confidence and calm.

National Crisis Hotline

If you're experiencing thoughts of self-harm or feeling overwhelmed call:

988
or
1-800-273-8255

Available 24/7 for support and guidance.

Remember: The pain you're experiencing right now is temporary, but your resilience and capacity for healing are permanent parts of who you are.

CHAPTER 10:

Beyond the Silence—Legacy, Estrangement, and Peace of Mind

WHEN A RELATIONSHIP WITH YOUR ADULT child becomes fractured or severed, the silence that follows can feel deafening. Yet within that silence lies an unexpected opportunity—the chance to create clarity, establish boundaries, and build a legacy that reflects your values and intentions, regardless of the current state of your family relationships.

Estate planning and financial preparation take on new dimensions when estrangement is part of your story. The traditional advice of "leave everything to the children" suddenly becomes complicated when communication has broken down, when trust has been damaged, or when you're uncertain about your child's well-being or intentions. You may find yourself asking difficult questions: How do I plan for someone who has cut me out of their life? What if reconciliation happens tomorrow, or never happens at all? How do I protect myself while still holding space for hope?

This chapter isn't about giving up on your relationship with your adult child—but as in previous chapters, it's about taking responsibility for the things you can control while that relationship remains uncertain. It's about creating financial security and peace of mind that doesn't depend on reconciliation, while still leaving room for the possibility that healing might come. Most importantly, it's about ensuring that your final wishes and values are clearly expressed, regardless of the current state of your family dynamics.

This chapter isn't meant to be an all-encompassing financial guide, but only as a guide as related to estrangement. Planning for an uncertain future requires both practical wisdom and emotional courage. It means facing the reality of estrangement while not letting that reality define every aspect of your future. It means protecting yourself without becoming bitter as well as preparing for various scenarios without losing hope.

Financial Planning with Flexibility

Creating financial security while staying flexible for future changes takes careful planning. Parents of estranged adult children often face a unique challenge: they need to prepare for an uncertain future while also handling present emotional and practical needs. This might include building a solid emergency fund to cover unexpected costs related to possible reconciliation—like therapy, travel, or helping a struggling child. At the same time, it's important not to lock into rigid financial plans that limit their ability to adapt. Smart strategies can include diversifying investments, keeping accessible savings, and using financial tools that offer both growth and flexibility. The aim is to build a strong, stable financial base that offers peace of mind and independence, while remaining open to future shifts in family dynamics.

Patricia shares her approach:

> *"I worked with my financial planner to create what we call a 'hope and reality' budget. It includes saving for retirement and my current needs while maintaining some resources for possible future family needs. This helps me feel both responsible and prepared for various possibilities."*

Key areas to address include:

- Retirement planning
- Investment strategies
- Insurance coverage
- Emergency funds

- Charitable giving
- Future care arrangements

Estate Planning and Legacy Considerations

When parents and their grown children aren't speaking to each other anymore, deciding what to leave them in a will becomes really hard. It's not just about money—it's about love, hurt feelings, and complicated family situations.

Many parents feel pulled in different directions. They still love their children even though they're not talking, but they're also deeply hurt by what happened. Some worry that leaving money might look like they're trying to control their kids even after they're gone. Others worry that leaving them nothing might make things worse forever. It gets even more complicated when there are grandchildren involved, or when the decision might affect other family members who still have a relationship with the estranged adult child.

There's no single "right" way to handle your will. Some parents decide to treat all their children equally in their will, no matter what's happening between them right now. Others choose to give less to the child they're not speaking with or put the money in a special account with rules about how it can be used. Some parents decide to give their money to charities or other people who have been there for them instead.

These are big decisions that deserve serious thought. It's smart to talk to both a lawyer who knows about wills and estates, and a counselor who can help work through the feelings involved. Remember, you can always change your will later if things change, and these money decisions don't have to fix all the relationship problems. The key is making a choice that feels right for your situation and values, not what others think you should do.

Legacy considerations might include:

- Updated will and estate documents
- Healthcare directives
- Legacy letters or recordings
- Charitable giving plans

- Personal history preservation
- Digital asset management

Patricia found peace in addressing these matters:

> *"Making these decisions was hard, but it helped me feel more in control of my future. I worked with both my attorney and therapist to create plans that felt right for my situation while leaving room for future changes."*

The Myth of Unconditional Love

Society often promotes the idea that parental love should be unconditional, including financial support. This myth can make parents feel guilty for setting boundaries or protecting themselves through estate planning. It's important to understand that love can be unconditional while still having appropriate boundaries and consequences.

Working with a therapist who understands family estrangement can help you process these complex emotions. Support groups for parents in similar situations can also provide validation and perspective.

Janet's journey:

> *"I spent months in therapy working through my guilt about removing my son from my will. My therapist helped me understand that protecting myself wasn't about punishing him—it was about honoring my own needs and the family members who have been there for me. It still hurts, but I have peace with my decision."*

Instead of viewing these decisions as failures or punishments, try reframing them as acts of self-care, boundary-setting, or protection of healthy relationships. Your estate planning can be an expression of your values and a way to support the people who have supported you.

Self-Compassion

Remember to be gentle with yourself throughout this process. Estate planning in the context of estrangement is not only a legal matter—it's an emotional and moral reckoning. It forces you to confront grief, disappointment, guilt, and love, often all at once. You may second-guess your choices, revisit old wounds, or wonder whether planning for the future means giving up hope for reconciliation. These are normal responses to this kind of heartbreak.

This is where self-compassion becomes essential. Giving yourself permission to prioritize your emotional safety and long-term peace is not selfish—it's survival. It means recognizing that you matter, that your well-being is worth protecting, and that it's okay to create boundaries even when they involve someone you love deeply.

Making estate decisions that reflect your current reality is not a betrayal of love—it's an acknowledgment of truth. Self-compassion allows you to hold space for the pain of estrangement while still making choices that honor your values, your healing, and your other relationships. It gives you room to say, "This is the best I can do with what I know right now," and to leave open the possibility of future change without sacrificing your present peace.

You don't need to get every detail perfect. What matters is that your decisions come from a place of clarity, not fear; love, not guilt; integrity, not obligation. In this way, estate planning becomes not a cold calculation, but a tender act of care—for yourself, for the people who've supported you, and for the future you're still courageously shaping.

Different Estate Strategies

Here are some examples that may resonate with your situation or inspire your own decision. These stories reflect the wide range of values, relationships, and intentions that shape estate planning in the context of estrangement. There is no one-size-fits-all answer—only the path that honors your truth, protects your peace, and upholds what matters most to you.

Eleanor chose this way to deal with her will:

> *"After years of silence from my son, I decided to leave my estate to a local mentorship program—I want my legacy to support young people who are trying to build something lasting."*

Lena felt relief after making her plans:

> "Removing my daughter from my will isn't about punishment—it's about love and realism. Her addiction brought years of chaos, and I couldn't risk enabling more harm. My therapist and I talked it through for months. In the end, I set up a fund for addiction recovery programs. That way, something good might still come from all the pain."

David made a choice that he felt worked for him, even from a distance:

> "Eric and I haven't spoken in decades. We disagreed on almost everything, and he walked away—but I kept him in the will. My lawyer asked if I was sure. I was. Maybe one day, this gesture will help heal what silence or words never could."

> **Legacy Planning Tips**
> - Work with qualified professionals.
> - Consider both emotional and practical impacts.
> - Build in flexibility where possible.
> - Keep documents accessible and updated.
> - Inform key support people of your wishes.
> - Review and revise periodically.

Cynthia and Dan's decision was made with thoughtful intention:

> "Everything we have is going to our three children who have made the effort to build strong relationships with us and who have allowed us to play a significant role in our grandchildren's lives. They have brought us so much joy, and we hope our legacy will help them continue that family closeness. Our estranged daughter currently isn't in our will. We will always love her, but right now, our connection is distant and uncertain. This decision celebrates and supports the relationships that are actively part of our lives today."

Thomas honored one of his strongest supporters:

> "I haven't heard from my son in years, but my niece Mallory is

> *always here when I need someone most. She doesn't show up out of obligation—she just cares. It feels right to leave everything to her, and my lawyer helped me write a letter to explain so it won't be contested."*

Sylvia gave her legacy to her values:

> *"I want my legacy to reflect who I am. My attorney helped me set up a donation to a literacy foundation. That's the story I want to leave behind—one of hope and learning."*

Remember: These decisions can be revisited and adjusted as circumstances change. The goal is creating clarity and peace of mind while maintaining appropriate flexibility.

Emotional and Relational Considerations

Estate planning decisions involving estrangement rarely affect only the immediate relationship. The ripple effects can touch siblings, extended family, and grandchildren in ways that may not be immediately apparent. Understanding these impacts helps you make more thoughtful decisions and prepare for potential consequences.

When you alter inheritance plans due to estrangement, remaining children may experience complex emotions. Some may feel relief that their consistent presence is being recognized, while others may feel burdened by guilt or worry about family judgment. Siblings might also fear that their inheritance comes with unspoken expectations to maintain family relationships or care for aging parents.

Your estate decisions can also affect relationships with in-laws, cousins, aunts, uncles, and family friends who maintain connections with your estranged child. Some extended family members may feel caught in the middle, unsure how to navigate relationships with both sides. Others may pressure you to "forgive and forget" or judge your decisions harshly.

Perhaps the most heartbreaking aspect involves grandchildren. When you're estranged from your adult child, you may have limited or no relationship with their children. Estate decisions must consider whether to include grandchildren despite the broken relationship with their parent, and how such decisions might affect the grandchildren's relationship with their own parent.

Linda reflects on her decision:

> *"When I removed my daughter from my will, I worried about my two grandchildren. I decided to set up education funds for them that can't be touched by their mother. It was important to me that they know I never stopped loving them, even though we can't have a relationship right now."*

Communication Strategies

Deciding whether and how to discuss your estate planning decisions requires careful consideration of your family dynamics, your goals, and potential consequences. Some parents choose full transparency, believing that open communication prevents surprises and allows family members to process the information over time. Others prefer privacy, feeling that their estate decisions are personal and shouldn't be influenced by others' opinions. Consider your family's communication style and your own comfort level with potential discussions or conflicts.

If you choose to share information, timing matters. Discussing estate plans during emotionally charged moments or family gatherings may not be ideal. Consider having individual conversations with key family members when emotions are calmer and you can have thoughtful discussions.

You might share general principles without specific details: "I want you to know that I've updated my estate planning to reflect current family relationships and my values." Or you might provide more specific information: "I've decided to divide my estate equally among my three children who maintain active relationships with me."

Consider having these conversations with a family therapist present, especially if emotions run high. A neutral professional can help facilitate discussions and ensure all parties feel heard while maintaining focus on your decision-making autonomy.

Marcus chose partial transparency:

> *"I told my two sons that I had updated my will to reflect our current family situation, but I didn't go into specifics. They understood what I meant. It opened the door for them to ask questions without me having to justify every decision."*

Handling Potential Challenges

Be prepared for family members who might try to influence your decisions through guilt, pressure, or emotional manipulation. Having clear boundaries about what you will and won't discuss helps protect your decision-making process.

The possibility of will contests or legal challenges adds another layer of complexity to estate planning when estrangement is involved. Keep in mind that not all unhappy family members can successfully contest a will, and rules change from state to state. Legal challenges typically require specific grounds such as lack of mental capacity, undue influence, fraud, or improper execution. Simply being unhappy with inheritance decisions usually isn't sufficient legal grounds for a successful contest.

Working with an experienced estate planning attorney to create documents that are less vulnerable to challenges helps you protect your right to choose. This might include:

- Detailed documentation of your mental capacity at the time of signing.
- Clear explanations of your reasoning in the will or accompanying letters.
- Witness testimonies about your decision-making process.
- Regular updates to show consistent decision-making over time
- No-contest clauses that reduce or eliminate inheritances for anyone who unsuccessfully challenges the will.

Keep records of the estrangement, including any attempts at communication, therapy records, or documentation of harmful behaviors. This evidence can support your decision-making rationale if challenged.

Having your attorney, doctor, or other professionals witness your decision-making process can provide valuable testimony if your mental capacity is questioned.

Sarah's precautions:

> "My attorney had me write a letter explaining my decisions and had it notarized. We also had my doctor confirm my mental capacity. I keep detailed records of my daughter's behavior and my attempts to reconcile. It's sad that I have to protect myself legally from my own child, but I need peace of mind."

The emotional weight of making estate planning decisions during estrangement cannot be understated. These decisions are among the most difficult any parent can face and often trigger intense feelings of grief, failure, and loss that need to be acknowledged and processed. Many parents experience guilt about their decisions, wondering if they're being too harsh, too protective, or too final. They may question whether they tried hard enough, forgave enough, or understood enough. This guilt can be paralyzing and prevent parents from making necessary decisions. You're not weak or selfish for struggling with these emotions. The complexity of loving someone while protecting yourself from their harmful behavior creates an impossible emotional situation that has no perfect solutions.

Permission to Change

Remember that estate planning documents can be updated if circumstances change. Giving yourself permission to make decisions based on current reality, while remaining open to future changes, can reduce some of the pressure and finality that makes these decisions so difficult.

Frances shares her experience with reconciliation and estate planning changes:

> "After the estrangement, I had removed my daughter from my will and my end-of-life choices. Things changed after seven years when she suddenly resurfaced, and we slowly rebuilt our

> *relationship. It took another two years of consistent contact and family therapy before I felt ready to update my documents again. I didn't rush it—I wanted to see real change and commitment from both of us. When I finally added her back to my will, it felt like a celebration of our healing, not just a legal document. My attorney helped me structure it so that her inheritance is contingent on our relationship remaining healthy. It gives me peace of mind while honoring the progress we've made."*

Guardianship and Care Decisions

When estrangement occurs, one of the most urgent decisions involves updating who will make medical and financial decisions if you become incapacitated. Many parents previously designated their adult child as their healthcare proxy or financial power of attorney, creating a vulnerable gap when that relationship breaks down.

Your healthcare proxy needs to be someone who understands your values, can handle medical decisions under pressure, and will advocate for your wishes. This person should be accessible, trustworthy, and emotionally stable enough to make difficult choices during a crisis. Consider naming a primary and backup person, ensuring both understand your preferences about end-of-life care, medical interventions, and quality-of-life decisions.

This person will manage your finances, pay bills, and make financial decisions if you're unable to do so. They need to be financially responsible, organized, and completely trustworthy with money. Some parents choose to split this role—having one person handle day-to-day finances and another manage investments or major decisions.

If you become incapacitated without proper documents in place, a court may need to appoint a guardian. This process can be expensive, time-consuming, and may result in someone you wouldn't choose making decisions for you. Clear, updated documents prevent this uncertainty.

Margaret shares her experience:

> *"After my daughter cut contact, I realized she was still my*

> *healthcare proxy. The thought of her making medical decisions while refusing to speak to me was terrifying. I updated everything to name my sister as primary and my best friend as backup. Both know my values and would fight for my wishes."*

Key steps include:

- Update all healthcare directives and power of attorney documents.
- Choose people who are geographically accessible and emotionally stable.
- Have detailed conversations about your preferences and values.
- Provide copies to your chosen advocates and your medical providers.
- Review and update these documents regularly.

Making clear guardianship and care decisions isn't just about legal protection—it's a powerful act of self-compassion. By thoughtfully choosing who will speak and act on your behalf, you remove uncertainty and reduce anxiety. This clarity allows you to focus more fully on healing, joy, and building the future you deserve. In taking care of these essential matters, you free up emotional space to live more peacefully now, knowing your well-being is securely in the hands of those who honor your values.

Digital Legacy Management

In our digital age, managing your online presence and digital assets after death requires specific planning. Without proper preparation, valuable digital assets can be lost forever, and online accounts may remain active indefinitely.

Most platforms offer legacy contact options or memorialization features. Facebook allows you to designate a legacy contact who can manage your account after death. Instagram offers account memorialization. LinkedIn profiles can be closed or memorialized. Review each platform's policies and set up appropriate legacy contacts.

Decide what happens to your digital content—photos, videos, documents, creative works. Do you want them preserved for family, donated to archives, or deleted? Some parents create digital memory books or recordings for future generations, while others prefer privacy.

Robert planned ahead:

> *"I spent a weekend organizing my digital life. I documented all my accounts, updated legacy contacts on social media, and moved important photos to a shared family cloud folder. My brother has the master password list. It gave me peace of mind knowing my digital chaos won't burden anyone."*

EXERCISE: Digital Asset Inventory

Create a comprehensive list of all digital accounts, including:

- Banking and investment accounts
- Social media profiles (Facebook, Instagram, Twitter, LinkedIn)
- Email accounts
- Cloud storage (Google Drive, Dropbox, iCloud)
- Digital photos and videos
- Online subscriptions and services
- Cryptocurrency wallets
- Digital creative works or intellectual property
- Passwords

Taking time now to organize your digital legacy is a meaningful act of care. It reduces confusion, prevents loss, and ensures your digital presence reflects your wishes. Whether you're preserving memories, protecting creative work, or simply easing the burden on loved ones, these steps are a modern extension of your legacy—one that honors both practicality and love.

Legacy Building Beyond Traditional Family

Many parents find meaning in creating legacies that extend beyond traditional family relationships. This might involve mentoring, community service, creative works, or other contributions that benefit others.

For example, when family estrangement changes your role as a grandparent, it's natural to feel a deep sense of loss. But many find new purpose by channeling their care and wisdom into community service. The nurturing energy once intended for grandchildren can instead support children, families, and neighbors in meaningful ways—offering healing, connection, and the chance to make a lasting impact.

Volunteering in schools, libraries, or community programs allows you to invest in the next generation. Whether you're reading to young children, mentoring teens, or helping with after-school tutoring, your presence can offer the consistency and encouragement many students need. There are also countless opportunities outside of formal education, such as supporting foster youth, leading summer camp activities, or helping families through faith-based or neighborhood initiatives.

Your support can extend directly to families who need it—babysitting for single parents, offering transportation, or serving as a grandparent figure to those without nearby relatives. Through both formal programs and informal connections, these efforts create powerful bonds and new traditions that grow from mutual respect and shared values, rather than obligation.

Most importantly, healing often emerges through these chosen relationships. The appreciation of a child you've mentored or a family you've helped can restore a sense of purpose and belonging. While these new bonds don't replace your family, they affirm that love, guidance, and legacy can thrive beyond biological ties. Start small, follow what calls to you, and trust that the good you do will ripple outward.

EXERCISE: Legacy Exploration

Consider:

- What wisdom have you gained?
- How might your experience help others?
- What contributions feel meaningful?
- What would you like to be remembered for?
- How can you share your gifts?

Remember: Your legacy isn't limited to family relationships—it includes all the ways you touch others' lives.

Looking Ahead with Courage and Peace

The journey of estrangement never follows a straight line. There will be moments of progress and setbacks, joy and grief, confidence and uncertainty. What matters is your commitment to continuing your story with courage and self-compassion.

Remember:

- Every small step toward healing matters.

- Joy and pain can coexist.
- Growth happens gradually.
- Support is always available.
- Your story continues to unfold.

You carry within you the strength to write new chapters of your life, filled with joy and purpose, while honoring all that has come before. Your journey continues, and every day offers fresh opportunities to choose growth, create meaning, and build resilience.

Life's most painful moments can lead to the greatest transformation. For parents, few things hurt more than being estranged from a child. But this pain doesn't have to mark the end of the story. Instead, it can be part of a continuing journey—one that you still shape every single day.

When you begin to see yourself not as a helpless victim of what happened, but as the author of your own life, it changes everything. You begin to recognize that the small choices you make each day matter: how you speak to yourself, how you care for your body, how you connect with others, and how you make sense of your pain.

These small, everyday decisions build into something greater—a path of healing, strength, and personal growth. While we may not be able to change our child's choices, we still have power over how we respond and who we become in the process.

Healing isn't something far away or final. It's something that happens now, in each moment of awareness and intention. This way of thinking shifts the focus from waiting—waiting for an apology, for reconnection, for peace—to actively living with meaning and purpose, right where we are right now.

Even deep pain can become the starting point for a new story—one of courage, wisdom, and a different kind of beauty, born not from having everything restored, but from rising above what was lost.

National Crisis Hotline

If you're experiencing thoughts of self-harm or feeling overwhelmed call:

988
or
1-800-273-8255

Available 24/7 for support and guidance.

Remember: Reaching out for help is a sign of strength and self-awareness.

NOTES

Chapter 1

Agllias, K. (2017). Family Estrangement: A Matter of Perspective. Routledge.

Agllias, K. (2018). Missing family: The emotional and physical health consequences of family estrangement. Journal of Social Work Practice, 32(4), 403-421.

Blake, L., Bland, B., & Golombok, S. (2015). Hidden Voices: Family Estrangement in Adulthood. University of Cambridge Centre for Family Research & Stand Alone.

Boss, P. (2016). Ambiguous Loss: Learning to Live with Unresolved Grief (2nd ed.). Harvard University Press.

Pillemer, K. (2020). Fault Lines: Fractured Families and How to Mend Them. Avery.

Scharp, K. M. (2016). Parent-Child Estrangement: Conditions for Communication and Making Amends. Journal of Family Communication, 16(3), 233-251.

Chapter 2

Agllias, K. (2018). Missing Family: Experiences of Family Estrangement in Adulthood. Journal of Social Work Practice, 32(1), 59-72.

Blake, L., Bland, B., & Golombok, S. (2015). Hidden Voices: Family Estrangement in Adulthood. University of Cambridge Centre for Family Research & Stand Alone.

Brown, B. (2012). Daring Greatly: How the Courage to Be Vulnerable Transforms the Way We Live, Love, Parent, and Lead. Gotham Books.

Boss, P. (2016). Ambiguous Loss: Learning to Live with Unresolved Grief (2nd ed.). Harvard University Press.

Coleman, J. (2020). Rules of Estrangement: Why Adult Children Cut Ties and How to Heal the Conflict. Harmony Books.

Neff, K. (2011). Self-Compassion: The Proven Power of Being Kind to Yourself. William Morrow.

Scharp, K. M. (2016). Parent-Child Estrangement: Conditions for Communication and Making Amends. Journal of Family Communication, 16(3), 233-251.

Chapter 3

Agllias, K. (2018). Family Estrangement: A Matter of Perspective. Routledge.

Blake, L., et al. (2015). Hidden Voices: Family Estrangement in Adulthood. University of Cambridge Centre for Family Research.

Boss, P. (2016). Ambiguous Loss: Learning to Live with Unresolved Grief. Harvard University Press.

Coleman, J. (2020). Rules of Estrangement: Why Adult Children Cut Ties and How to Heal the Conflict. Harmony Books.

Pillemer, K. (2020). Fault Lines: Fractured Families and How to Mend Them. Avery Publishing.

Scharp, K. M. (2019). You're Not Crazy, You're Not Wrong: Understanding the Mother Experience of Parental Estrangement. Journal of Family Communication, 19(2), 191-219.

Siegel, D. J. (2020). The Developing Mind: How Relationships and the Brain Interact to Shape Who We Are. The Guilford Press.

Chapter 4

Bolton, G. (2011). Write Yourself: Creative Writing and Personal Development. Jessica Kingsley Publishers.

DeSalvo, L. (2000). Writing as a Way of Healing: How Telling Our Stories Transforms Our Lives. Beacon Press.

Lepore, S.J., & Smyth, J.M. (2015). The Writing Cure: How Expressive Writing Promotes Health and Emotional Well-Being. American Psychological Association.

Pennebaker, J.W., & Smyth, J.M. (2016). Opening Up by Writing It Down: How Expressive Writing Improves Health and Eases Emotional Pain. The Guilford Press.

Thompson, K. (2010). Therapeutic Journal Writing: An Introduction for Professionals. Jessica Kingsley Publishers.

Chapter 5

Agllias, K. (2017). Family Estrangement: A Matter of Perspective. Routledge.

Blake, L. (2017). Hidden Voices: Family Estrangement in Adulthood. University of Cambridge Centre for Family Research.

Boss, P. (2016). The Context and Process of Theory Development: The Story of Ambiguous Loss. Journal of Family Theory & Review, 8(3), 269-286.

Coleman, J. (2020). Rules of Estrangement: Why Adult Children Cut Ties and How to Heal the Conflict. Harmony Books.

Pillemer, K. (2020). Fault Lines: Fractured Families and How to Mend Them. Avery.

Scharp, K. M., & Thomas, L. J. (2021). Family Estrangement: A Communication Perspective. Lexington Books.

Chapter 6

Agllias, K. (2017). Family Estrangement: A Matter of Perspective.

Boss, P. (2016). Loss, Trauma, and Resilience: Therapeutic Work with Ambiguous Loss.

Coleman, J. (2020). Rules of Estrangement: Why Adult Children Cut Ties and How to Heal the Conflict.

Neff, K. (2011). Self-Compassion: The Proven Power of Being Kind to Yourself.

Pillemer, K. (2020). Fault Lines: Fractured Families and How to Mend Them.

Chapter 7

Agllias, K. (2017). Family Estrangement: A Matter of Perspective. Routledge.

Blake, L., Bland, B., & Edge, D. (2015). The Hidden Voices Project: Experiences of Estrangement. University of Cambridge Press.

Coleman, J. (2020). Rules of Estrangement: Why Adult Children Cut Ties and How to Heal the Conflict. Harmony Books.

Pillemer, K. (2020). Fault Lines: Fractured Families and How to Mend Them. Avery.

Scharp, K. M. (2019). Family Communication and Estrangement: Research, Theory, and Practice. Routledge.

Scharp, K. M., & Thomas, L. J. (2016). Family "bonds": Making meaning of parent–child relationships in estrangement narratives. Journal of Family Communication, 16(1), 32-50.

Stand Alone. (2018). Understanding Family Estrangement in Adulthood. Stand Alone Research Report.

Chapter 8

Agllias, K. (2017). *Family Estrangement: A Matter of Perspective*. Routledge.

Blake, L., Bland, B., & Edge, D. (2015). *The Hidden Voices Project: Experiences of Estrangement*. University of Cambridge Press.

Pillemer, K. (2020). *Fault Lines: Fractured Families and How to Mend Them*. Avery.

Coleman, J. (2020). *Rules of Estrangement: Why Adult Children Cut Ties and How to Heal the Conflict*. Harmony Books.

Chapter 9

Boss, P. (2006). *Loss, Trauma, and Resilience: Therapeutic Work With Ambiguous Loss*. W. W. Norton & Company.

Coleman, J. (2020). *Rules of Estrangement: Why Adult Children Cut Ties and How to Heal the Conflict*. Random House.

McGregor, S. (2016). *Done With The Crying: Help and Healing for Mothers of Estranged Adult Children*. Familius.

ABOUT THE AUTHOR

Anna Strand is a mother who has endured the sudden inexplicable estrangement of an adult child, who also abandoned the rest of the large family and extended family. Thankfully, her other children are fantastically supportive, and she is the grandmother all their kids want to play with. Going to Grandma's is always an adventure, and Anna plans to keep it that way.

www.ingramcontent.com/pod-product-compliance
Lightning Source LLC
LaVergne TN
LVHW051548070426
835507LV00021B/2461